"Mount Rainier offers the finest glacier climbing in the lower 48 states. This book offers keen insight into exploring the complexities of its routes."

> George Dunn, Master Guide, Rainier Mountaineering, Inc.
> Currently has more climbs of Mount Rainier than any
> other person in history: 390.

"Mount Rainier offers dozens of great routes to the adventurous intermediate climber equipped with proper skills and good judgment. Climbing Mount Rainier: The Essential Guide *will help you explore them."*

> Eric Simonson, veteran Mount Rainier guide and
> co-owner, Mount Rainier Alpine Guides

"The best guidebooks are those written by climbers who have an intimate knowledge of a particular area. Both Alex and Fred fit that description and they have written a book that will well serve climbers wishing to explore Rainier's varied routes. The many photos add greatly to their already clear route descriptions. Rainier National Park's centennial year is an excellent time to climb The Mountain and an opportune time to have this new guidebook available."

> Phil Ershler, Assistant Chief Guide, Rainier Mountaineering, Inc.
> and co-owner, International Mountain Guides

Climbing
Mount Rainier

The Essential Guide

ALPEN BOOKS PRESS

Climbing
Mount Rainier

The Essential Guide

Fred Beckey
&
Alex Van Steen

ALPEN
BOOKS
PRESS

Published by
AlpenBooks Press, LLC
3616 South Road, C-1
Mukilteo, WA 98275 USA

First edition, 1999

Manufactured in the United States of America

Dedication by Van Steen

To my old friends, Lee James and Billy Zink,
and to the motivated climber in us all.

Editor: Christine Clifton-Thornton
Maps: Green Rhino Graphics
Cover design: Lily Pad Productions
Book design & layout: Green Rhino Graphics

Cover photograph: *Mount Rainier's dramatic northwest face.* (Jason Edwards)
Frontispiece: *RMI guide Cate Casson leads a group up the flank of Disappointment Cleaver on a cold and windy day in 1997.* (Alex Van Steen)

ISBN 0-9669795-0-8

Contents

Warning

CLIMBING IS A DANGEROUS ACTIVITY, ONE IN WHICH YOU CAN GET SERIOUSLY INJURED OR DIE.

READ BELOW BEFORE YOU USE ANY INFORMATION IN THIS BOOK!

This guidebook contains information provided by the authors and other climbers. Reasonable attempts have been made to check the information for accuracy, however, complete accuracy cannot be assured. Areas where there may be errors or omissions include route descriptions, maps, route photos, climbing times, difficulty ratings, etc. Additionally, information such as difficulty ratings, climbing times, safety measures, etc. are subjective and are based on the experiences of well-trained, physically fit climbers, which you may not be.

In addition to the inaccuracies that are associated with writing a climbing guidebook, there are the dangers associated with the climbing activity. Such dangers include, but are not limited to: changing snow and ice characteristics; crevasses; avalanche; loose rock or rockfall; mudslide; volcanic eruption; sudden weather changes; lightning; equipment failures; fatigue; hypothermia; altitude sickness; etc.

Because of these factors, you must exercise your own judgement on whether you should climb the mountain and whether a particular route is suitable for one at your level of skill and preparation. Do not climb unless you've had climbing instruction and climbing experience. Make sure you are in good enough physical condition for the climb. Make sure you have the right equipment, and that it is in proper condition.

And you should use your own judgement as to whether the route descriptions make sense. Do not depend on any information found in this book for your personal safety. Talk to other climbers who have been on the route you want to take, at the time you want to take it. If you climb a route and start to have some doubt as to where it goes, or you start to have difficulty, or the weather looks suspect, back off and reevaluate the climb.

To sum up, you use this book entirely at your own risk.

THERE ARE NO WARRANTIES, EITHER EXPRESSED OR IMPLIED, THAT THIS GUIDEBOOK IS ACCURATE, OR THAT THE INFORMATION CONTAINED HEREIN IS RELIABLE. YOUR USE OF THIS GUIDEBOOK INDICATES YOUR ASSUMPTION OF RISK THAT IT MAY CONTAIN ERRORS OR OMISSIONS AND IS YOUR ACKNOWLEDGMENT THAT YOU ASSUME SOLE RESPONSIBILITY FOR YOUR CLIMBING SAFETY.

AlpenBooks Press, LLC

Mount Rainier:
Overall Area Map

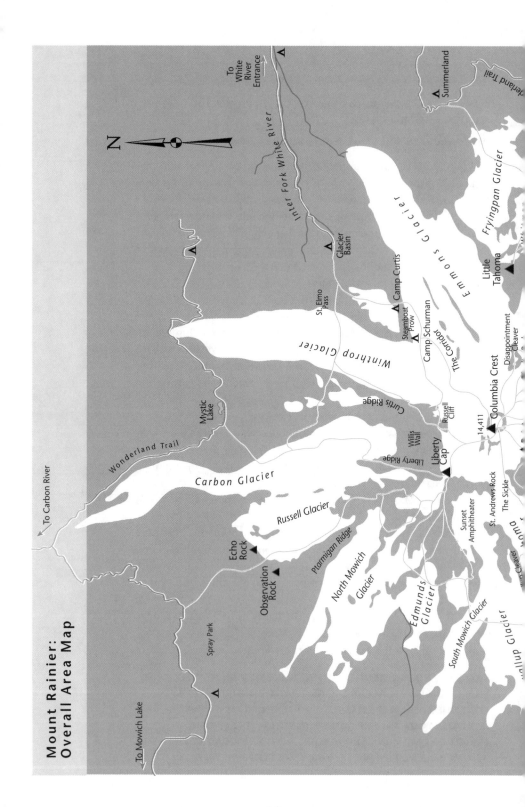

N

To Carbon River

To Mowich Lake

Spray Park

Wonderland Trail

Mystic Lake

To White River Entrance

Inter Fork White River

Glacier Basin

St. Elmo Pass

Camp Curtis

Steamboat Prow

Camp Schurman

The Corridor

Winthrop Glacier

Emmons Glacier

Summerland

Fryingpan Glacier

Little Tahoma

Disappointment Cleaver

Curtis Ridge

Willis Wall

Russell Cliff

Liberty Ridge

Liberty Cap

Columbia Crest

14,411

Carbon Glacier

Russell Glacier

Echo Rock

Observation Rock

Ptarmigan Ridge

North Mowich Glacier

Edmunds Glacier

South Mowich Glacier

Sunset Amphitheater

St. Andrews Rock

The Sickle

Wallup Glacier

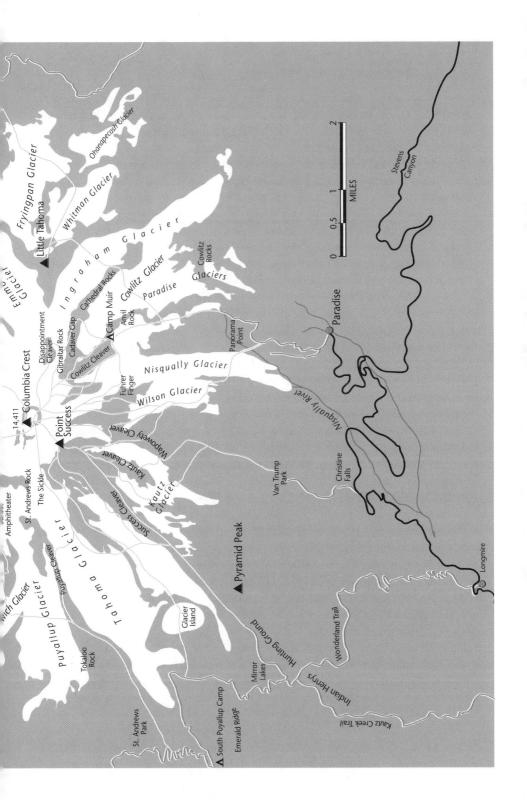

Fryingpan Glacier

Little Tahoma

Ohanapecosh Glacier

Whitman Glacier

Emmel Glacier

Ingraham Glacier

Disappointment Cleaver

Gibraltar Rock

Cadaver Gap

Cowlitz Cleaver

Cathedral Rocks

Camp Muir

Anvil Rock

Cowlitz Glacier

Paradise Glaciers

Cowlitz Rocks

Columbia Crest

14,411

Point Success

Nisqually Glacier

Führer Finger

Wilson Glacier

Panorama Point

Paradise

Amphitheater

St. Andrews Rock

The Sickle

Wapowety Cleaver

Kautz Cleaver

Success Cleaver

Kautz Glacier

Van Trump Park

Christine Falls

Nisqually River

Pyramid Peak

Tahoma Glacier

Puyallup Glacier

Puyallup Cleaver

wich Glacier

Glacier Island

Tokaloo Rock

St. Andrews Park

South Puyallup Camp

Emerald Ridge

Mirror Lakes

Hunting Ground

Indian Henrys

Kautz Creek Trail

Wonderland Trail

Longmire

Stevens Canyon

0   0.5   1   2

MILES

More than any other mountain I've climbed, Mount Rainier has meant the most to me. Why not Mount McKinley or K2, to name just two others? Just as a person never forgets the first time he fell in love, the first big mountain he focuses on in childhood will remain etched in his memory.

Outside of Alaska, Rainier is the country's highest freestanding mountain, visible from miles around. But where I grew up in eastern Washington, you had to go a few miles south of town before you could see the tip of Rainier's summit peeking over the top of the hills that stretched along the Columbia River. On infrequent trips to Seattle as a youngster, I always felt a thrill of anticipation as my father drove our family over those intervening hills. On the last rise, Mount Rainier sprang into view, its entire upper mass towering above the surrounding landscape. But I didn't think of climbing the mountain then; it seemed too big, too majestic.

I got my first chance to climb Rainier the summer I turned twenty, when my high school friend and classmate, Fred Dunham, and I were invited to help a slightly older, more experienced climber who had been hired by the Park Service to go to the summit to clean up a glaciological research campsite. Our plan was to camp on the summit, but an incoming storm forced us down after our work was completed. It would not be the last time that atrocious weather would turn a pleasant experience on Mount Rainier into a struggle for survival.

One of my early mentors was the great White Pass climber Dave Mahre. In the early 1960s, Willis Wall, the treacherous 3,600-foot-high precipice on the mountain's north side, was the most coveted objective. Although widely considered a death-trap, Mahre believed that one of the three ribs splitting the massive face would provide a safe route two-thirds of the way up, allowing access to the nearly vertical rock band separating the two 300-foot-high icecliffs that rimmed the top.

In the race to become the first to climb Willis Wall, in 1963 I joined Mahre and two others for an attempt. Under ideal conditions we climbed the proposed route to the top of the wall. The crux was the "traverse of the angels," a narrow, exposed catwalk between the two icecliffs. Near Liberty Cap we became disoriented in one of those whiteouts that typically plague climbers high on the mountain. One of my companions was in the early stages of pulmonary edema, which forced us to descend quickly. Completely by chance we descended the Mowich Face, a route climbed only once before.

It wasn't until years later that we learned we were not the first to climb Willis Wall. That distinction went to Charlie Bell, an unheralded solo climber who astounded the local climbing community with his audacious claim. He'd only been on the flanks of Liberty Ridge, the critics said. Charlie didn't carry a camera on his 1961 climb, and when substantial doubts were raised he came back a year later with a camera. Even then, Bell's photographs were inconclusive until they could be compared to those that Alex Bertulis and I took on our 1970 winter ascent of the westernmost rib. Although his photographs documented only his climb of the upper part of our route, the climbing community eventually accepted Bell's claim of the earlier complete ascent.

I did two other climbs of Willis Wall. The last, in 1974, was a delightful romp up a new line between the east and central ribs with Dusan Jagersky, but the one that preceded it nearly cost me my life. In 1971 Ed Boulton and I made the second ascent of the central rib. Caught in a fierce storm just below Liberty Cap, I became hypothermic during our second bivouac on the climb. Without Ed's assistance, I wouldn't have made it down. That bivouac experience, and others like it on Rainier, was crucial to my survival years later near the summit of K2. What it taught me was that no matter how cold and miserable you may be, morning *will* come.

Rainier offers far more to climbers than Willis Wall. There are nearly fifty routes on the mountain. Aside from the two most popular, easy ones—Disappointment Cleaver and the Emmons Glacier—most of the others are seldom attempted. That's a shame, because there's nothing like having a route to yourself on Rainier. It's still possible to have a wilderness experience just around the corner from hundreds of climbers. The choice is yours.

For those who aspire to reach the summit of Mount Rainier as the stepping stone to bigger, more difficult mountains, history validates these ambitions. If you do well on Rainier, you are likely to do well on Mount McKinley or Aconcagua. Beyond that, the Himalayas—and Mount Everest—beckon. The snow, ice, winds, storms, white-out conditions, and moderate high altitude of Rainier are all grist for the mill of the greater ranges of the world. Dozens of successful Everest climbers got their start on Rainier.

This guidebook should provide a handy source to those who are willing to create their own Rainier adventure. Just remember that the mountain can turn on you in an incredibly short period of time. Watch for those telltale cloud wisps blowing in from the southwest. By all means, go for the summit. But have the good judgement to turn around when it makes sense to do so. Good climbing!

> *Jim Wickwire*
> Seattle
> January 1999

An Invitation to Climb

"Climb the mountains and get their good tidings. Nature's peace will flow into you as sunshine flows into trees. The winds will blow their own freshness into you, and the storms their energy, while cares will drop off like autumn leaves."

John Muir

Acknowledgments

Alex Van Steen

We have been privileged with assistance from so many people to make this project possible. Fred and I couldn't do it all, nor would we try to. Many thanks to Jim Wickwire for authoring the Foreword. Not only has he long been one of my personal heroes, but his pioneering accomplishments on Mount Rainier are a yardstick by which countless other explorers measure their progress and set their sights. I also wish to thank Eric Simonson, Jason Edwards, Art Rausch, Craig John, Jim Yoder, Ned Randolph, Ruth Mahre, Dave Mahre and Peter Whittaker for their assistance and contributions to the text. My wife, Ruth Ann Van Steen, spent countless hours keying and editing the initial versions of the text. Without her, I couldn't have tackled this project so energetically. Fred and I are certainly very fortunate to have been given the use of photographs taken by so many people who generously donated their pictures to the guidebook. Photos were contributed by Eric Simonson, Joe Catellani, Dan Davis, Len Kannapell, Don Goodman, Jim Nelson, Alex Bertulis, Jeff Chichester, Dan Goering, Gary Glenn, George Dunn, Terry LaFrance, Mike Lobosco, Heather Macdonald, and Mike Hattrup. Very special thanks to Tom Stewart and Jason Edwards, who provided a large number of photographs, sharing with us their great love for Mount Rainier. Additionally, professional photographers Joe Stermitz, Barry Gregg, Ed Cooper, Bob and Ira Spring, and Jim Stuart graciously contributed spectacular photos. Both the Geophysical Institute of the University of Alaska Fairbanks, which has custody of the U.S. Geological Survey glacier photographs, and the Boeing Company are to be acknowledged for making aerial pictures available. Thanks to the American Alpine Club of Canada for permission to use information from their publications. Finally, a special note of thanks to Craig Van Hoy for originally hooking Fred and me up together to start work on this project.

Introduction

From near and far, Mount Rainier has a looming presence. When only partially visible through clouds the mountain may appear suspended, almost dreamlike, over the Puget Sound Lowland. Seen at dawn through a ground fog, it may appear spectral. On a clear day the mountain, from its peak to the shoulders sloping into surrounding hills, may seem close enough to walk over and touch. It may be brilliantly white when struck by the reflecting rays of the sun, or gloomy and gray when its summit is made invisible by a cloudcap. Regardless of the weather—clear, cloudy, or foggy—the impact of 14,411-foot Mount Rainier (only 65 miles from Seattle's waterfront) is immediate and breathtaking.

Early Native Americans saw this volcano as part of their spiritual life, a godlike icon, a singular beacon dominating the landscape. Today, thousands of years later, residents of the region and travelers are still inspired and challenged by the glacier-clad mountain.

A mountain of majesty and menace, Mount Rainier has a treacherous grandeur, one not always apparent to the distant viewer, who may see its glittering snow and ice as a pretty crystal soaring out of the evergreen lowlands. Such a cloak of serenity hides the eruptive danger within this old but active member of the volcanic Cascade Range. Mount Rainier's relative accessibility to nearby communities further lulls the public with an illusion of permanency. It is worth noting, however, that this mighty volcano poses a threat to the people in its shadow, even as it lures alpinists to its slopes.

Ever since the first serious attempt to reach the summit in 1857, the great mountain has thrown down an irresistible challenge for the adventurous. The mountain's exploration and the early ascents form one of the great sagas of a quest to master the unknown—a fascinating period of history played out amid the throes of immigration and settlement in the Pacific Northwest.

The Native Americans who for ages revered the mountain applied the name *Tahoma*—or a quite similar word with different spellings—which may have been a generic term applied to all snow peaks. But not long after Capt. George Vancouver of the Royal Navy sailed through the Strait of Juan de Fuca, he named "the round snowy mountain" after his friend, Rear Admiral Peter Rainier. In 1810 Vancouver published the name Rainier in his journal in London, initiating a controversy that lasted for over a century.

John Muir

Like Thoreau, Muir was a paragon of nature worship. As surely as Picasso changed art, Muir directed political views toward nature preservation.

The passionate Muir became involved with many aspects of wilderness and earth science. Although Muir dallied with climbing at times, his greatest accomplishments were long hikes (he once walked from Wisconsin to Florida, and he became the pioneer hiker of the Sierra Nevada).

In 1888, with Philemon Van Trump as guide, Muir took part on the fourth ascent of Mount Rainier. Muir's accounts of the ascent and Arthur C. Warner's photographs earned fame for the mountain. Only a year later President William McKinley designated Mount Rainier National Park.

At a high camp not far from present Camp Muir, the man who would become America's most eloquent spokesman for the majesty of wilderness recalled that the wind "drove gritty ashes and fragments of pumice about our ears while chilling us to the bone."

Muir, the founder of the Sierra Club, belonged to no formal religious

15

In later years a movement arose to restore the native name. Amid agitation from citizens of Tacoma, who claimed the native name should prevail over Vancouver's discovery from the sea in 1792, petitions were made to change the name. Ultimately, the Board of Geographic Names found that the name Rainier was firmly fixed by right of discovery and priority of the international usage, and, for better or worse, Vancouver's tribute to his friend remains.

Volcanism and Eruptions

There is a ferocious power pent up beneath the surface of the restless earth. Magmas from the mantle (the layer of hot rock comprising the bulk of the earth) emerge at ocean-floor ridges and also at breaks in the earth's thin outer crust. When rocks of a descending plate at a continental margin become partially molten and buoyant with heat, magma rises. When magma moves toward the earth's surface at weak spots, it may erupt erratically in the active subduction zone in the form of stratovolcanoes. Examples of such volcanoes are Mount Rainier, Mount St. Helens, Mount Hood, Mount Shasta, El Pico de Orizaba, and the chain of Katmai volcanoes in Alaska.

Mount Rainier is a part of the Pacific Ocean's "Ring of Fire." It stands midway in a line of volcanoes from Lassen Peak in California to Mount Garibaldi in British Columbia. Off the coastline of the Pacific Northwest, a slow, grinding descent of a slab of ocean crust, the Juan de Fuca plate, dives beneath the continent. As this plate dives (a subduction), it triggers the melting of rock into magma, which for at least 200,000 years has risen to the surface to form the various Cascade Range volcanoes.

Danger lurks within Mount Rainier. The great 1980 explosion of Mount St. Helens gave the Northwest a grim demonstration of how hot, molten magma, simmering beneath the continental crust, can violently erupt. The great detonation of Mount Katmai in Alaska (a three-day explosion) in 1912 is indicative of the volcanic power of destruction. That detonation created a vast, lifeless valley (the Valley of Ten Thousand Smokes) from a red-hot lava flow and left a crater larger than Crater Lake in Oregon. While the Katmai explosion occurred in an uninhabited region, a similar eruption, that of Mont Pelée in the populated West Indies, killed some 30,000 people. When the Indonesian volcano Krakatoa blew out its heart, volcanic dust caused a sky of inky blackness, and the blast was even heard in distant Australia.

Mount Rainier was once considerably higher and of greater bulk. In centuries past, it built up its cone with the materials ejected by its own eruptions, perhaps reaching 16,000 feet in altitude through successive lava flows and explosions of rock débris. Geologists have pointed to such evidence as steeply dipping lava flows, particularly those on Gibraltar, the Sunset Amphitheater, and the South Tahoma Headwall (these flows slant upward toward an earlier, higher vent). Such colorful volcanic layers act as a natural filing system, preserving the record of lava deposition.

With Point Success and Liberty Cap on the summit rim as remnants on the side of a higher cone, the present summit area also gives evidence of a former, higher summit. At times, heat deep inside the volcano also caused great devastation on flanking walls. Such heat can explain an inward collapse of the summit region and the production of a vast crater. The collapse truncated a higher summit. Great mudflows caused by violent eruptions, hydrothermal alteration of rock, and heat diminished Mount Rainier's bulk and appearance.

Mount Rainier has long displayed a pattern of violence. If past volcanic chaos is duplicated, Mount Rainier could well become a mountain of great turmoil. With but little notice, the volcano could take on a lethal persona and become animated from its present dormancy.

Geologists and emergency management personnel have ample reason to be apprehensive, mindful of such Rainier events as the Osceola Mudflow, a gigantic lahar that swept into the lowlands almost to Tacoma some 5,800 years ago. The more recent Electron Mudflow seared the landscape nearly to Puyallup only some 500 years ago. The settlement pattern has changed drastically in just the past few decades. Within 30 miles of Mount Rainier there is a swelling population and new commerce. Towns such as Enumclaw, Auburn, Bonney Lake, and Puyallup are all susceptible to the whims of the earth's internal processes.

Geologists point out that at least 100,000 people reside on débris once washed down by Mount Rainier's dangerous lahars. The risk of devastation is increased because of the mountain's glaciers; the melting of any portion of these could occur from subterranean heat.

creed, yet forests and mountains formed his temple. In one of his numerous essays about his beloved Sierra Nevada, he observed that "the scriptures of the ancient glaciers cover every rock, mountain, and valley of the range." One year after climbing to Rainier's summit, Muir took part in the grandiose Harriman Alaska Expedition, where he studied the natural features of Glacier Bay (later, the Muir Glacier was named in his honor).

Although Muir was not penniless, he turned his back on financial rewards. Once when asked about the magnate Harriman's wealth, Muir replied, "Why, I am richer than Harriman. I have all the money I want and he hasn't."

Glaciers

Mount Rainier is almost completely smothered in glaciers. Six bodies of ice flow radially from the summit icecap, together with other glaciers, covering some 33 square miles—the most on any single mountain in the United States, excluding Alaska.

The glaciers that emanate from the summit icecap are the Emmons, Winthrop, Tahoma, Kautz, Nisqually, and Ingraham. Other significant glaciers, such as the Carbon, Wilson, South Tahoma, and both Mowich Glaciers, begin the zone of greatest ice sculpting, between 10,000 and 12,000 feet.

Between the principal glaciers are secondary "inter" glaciers, bodies of ice nourished wholly by snowfall. Examples are the disappearing Paradise, Van Trump, Russell and Fryingpan Glaciers.

There has been vast glacier shrinkage in the Cascade Range within the past few hundred years. The Tahoma Glacier, which cascades down the western flank of Mount Rainier, extended over 1 mile farther down valley in the 1830s. The Nisqually, nearly 4 miles in length and the largest glacier on the south flank, like other glaciers, has responded drastically to climate variations. In approximately 1836 it extended 600 feet below the bridge on the road to Paradise and filled the valley wall. The glacier has now retreated to well above the bridge, to an altitude of about 4,800 feet.

The Carbon Glacier embodies the most primeval glacial world. It is nourished by falling ice and by direct snowfall into its enormous hollowed cirque. The cold barricade of this northern face is surely unique within the alpine regions of the Pacific Northwest.

The Climbing Season

Generally stable weather and good route conditions make summer the most popular time for climbing Mount Rainier. May and even June can be plagued with considerable precipitation and subsequent avalanche hazard. Rainier usually sees its last spring storm about the time the Fourth of July rolls around, and July and August are often superb climbing months. Occasionally in August the freezing level rises as warm moist weather systems move in off the Pacific Ocean, causing rain high on the mountain. A subsequent drop in the freezing level then leaves the mountain coated with a thin skeleton of ice, to cause very treacherous conditions. By late August the fall storms begin arriving, but the mountain is often climbable well into October. The risks of open crevasses and rockfall are definitely higher in the fall. November doesn't see much activity on the upper mountain, primarily because crevasses open widest at that time, and also because the guide service on the Paradise flank of the mountain shuts down for the season. Skiers can still enjoy the lower mountain, especially the easily accessible Muir Snowfield above Paradise. The occasional high-pressure systems that move across Washington at this time of year may also give the motivated climber an opportunity to squeak in a route, especially ridge routes like Gibraltar Ledge or Success Cleaver, although avalanche hazard usually remains high to extreme.

Climbing Services in the Park

For professionally guided climbs of Mount Rainier, the following guide services are available.

Rainier Mountaineering, Inc. (RMI)
535 Dock Street, Suite 209
Tacoma, WA 98402
(360) 569-2227 (summer) or (253) 627-6242 (winter)
http://www.rmiguides.com

RMI, established in 1968, offers a one-day basic techniques class, a crevasse rescue class, two-day climbs of the Disappointment Cleaver and Ingraham Glacier routes, five-day Camp Muir Seminars, five-day Expedition Seminars, and Winter Expedition Seminars. The Expedition Seminars climb the mountain via one of several available routes (Kautz Glacier, Fuhrer Finger, Gibraltar Ledge, and more) and are the training

RMI guides George Dunn and Curtis Fawley, and climber Barbara Boulton sign the summit register. *(Jason Edwards)*

seminars upon which most others in the country are modeled.

In addition to RMI, there are at present several other guide services operating on Mount Rainier. The guide services listed below are expected to be issued business permits for operation in 1999 by the National Park Service. All these guide services offer one form or another of a four-day summit climb via the Emmons Glacier route, as well as other related adventures (e.g., crevasse rescue classes, avalanche courses, and ski circumnavigations). No other guide services operate legally within the park boundaries.

Mount Rainier Alpine Guides, LLC
(Operated by Eric Simonson and Paul Baugher, both longtime veterans of Mount Rainier)
P.O. Box T
Ashford, WA 98304
(360) 569-0977
email: alpine@mashell.com
http://www.climbnet.com/rainier/index.html

Cascade Alpine Guides, LLC
P.O. Box 40563
Bellevue, WA 98015-4563
(425) 688-8054
(800) 981-0381
email: info@cascadealpine.com
http://www.cascadealpine.com

American Alpine Institute, Ltd.
1515 12th Street
Bellingham, WA 98225
(360) 671-1505
email: aai@aai.cc
http://www.aai.cc/programs/rainier.htm

Alpine Ascents International, Inc.
121 Mercer Street
Seattle, WA 98109
(206) 378-1927
email: aaiclimb@accessone.com
http://www.mountainzone.com/aai

Transportation to the Park

Mount Rainier National Park has seven entrances (although only three are used for the route approaches) and is accessible from several directions. Most climbers visiting the area for the first time fly in to Seattle–Tacoma International Airport ("Sea–Tac"), just a few miles south of Seattle, but there are many transporation options available.

Air. Direct flights can be taken to Seattle and Portland from most major cities of the world.

Rail. AMTRAK provides rail service with stops in Seattle, Tacoma, Centralia, and Portland on north-to-south routes, and Seattle, Auburn, Ellensburg, and Yakima on east-to-west routes.

Bus. *Greyhound/Trailways* (phone (800) 426-7505), provides bus service to the major cities and towns in the area. *Gray Line Worldwide* (phone (800) 994-7295) in Seattle and Tacoma offers tours to the park every day from May 1 through October 11. *Rainier Shuttle* (phone (360) 569-2331), based out of Ashford, Washington, provides shuttle van service from Sea–Tac Airport to the Nisqually Entrance and Paradise, with several accommodating stops along the way. It operates daily through the summer season and in conjunction with Rainier Mountaineering, Inc.'s Winter Expedition Seminars in the winter. *Rainier Overland Transportation Company* (phone (360) 569-2604), also out of Ashford, provides shuttle van service from the Sea–Tac Airport to various points in the park, including custom trips to numerous trailheads.

Personal vehicles and rental cars. Rentals are available at Sea–Tac Airport and in Yakima and Portland. Be aware that no gasoline is available inside the park. For most roads, opening and closing dates vary depending on snow conditions, and most are open only during the summer season (from Memorial Day to early October). One exception is the Nisqually Entrance, which remains open all year. Even then, vehicle access is limited to the 18 miles between the entrance and Paradise, between November and May. Because access to Mount Rainier is often

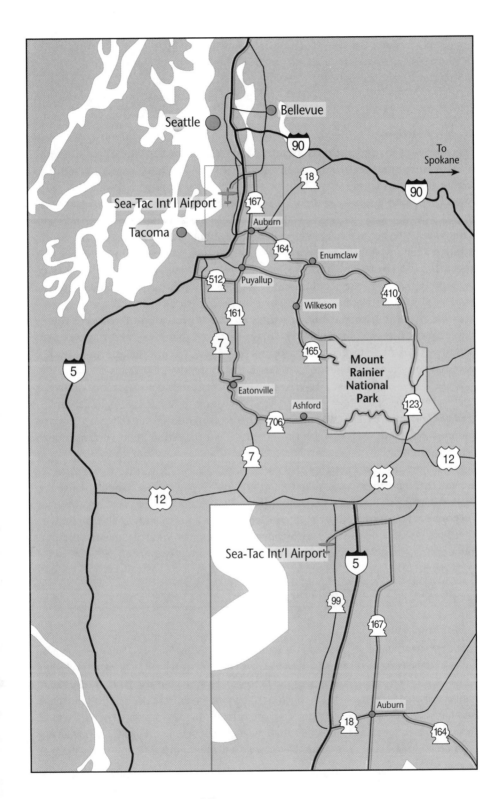

impaired as roads wash out or become snowbound, it is best to contact park headquarters at Tahoma Woods in advance (phone (360) 569-2211).

Visitation is always highest on summer weekends and holidays. On sunny summer weekends, large crowds arrive early and parking lots at most popular areas, such as Paradise and Sunrise, generally fill quickly.

Driving Directions

From Sea–Tac International Airport to the Nisqually Entrance: From Highway 99 alongside Sea–Tac Airport (where rental cars are located), access I-5 south to Highway 18 east (about 12 miles). In a few miles, exit onto Highway 167 south (toward Puyallup). As you approach Puyallup, stay in the right-hand lanes to enter Highway 512 west. Continue on Highway 512 for several miles and take the Eatonville/161 South exit. Turn left (and go south) on Meridian Avenue (161 South) through its many stoplights. Another half hour brings you to Eatonville. Beware, as speed limits are strictly enforced in Eatonville. Follow signs to Mount Rainier. Eventually, SR 706 (the Mountain Highway) leads you through Ashford to the Nisqually Entrance. Paradise is another 18 miles up Park Road.

From Sea–Tac International Airport to the White River Entrance: Follow the previous directions to Highway 18. Go eastward to Auburn and Highway 164. Follow Highway 164 to the town of Enumclaw (about 15 miles). Take Highway 410 east and continue south about 38 miles to the White River Entrance.

From Yakima to Paradise: Travel west on US 12, then north along SR 123 to the Stevens Canyon Entrance (open only in summer). Follow the signs to Paradise, 21 miles farther.

From Yakima to the White River Entrance: Follow SR 410 west (crossing Chinook Pass) and then travel north on SR 123 to the White River Entrance (open only in summer).

From Portland to Paradise: Follow I-5 north to US 12 east (to Mossyrock). At Morton, head north on SR 7, then east at Elbe on SR 706 to the Nisqually Entrance. Follow the signs 18 miles to Paradise.

From Portland to Rainier's east side: Follow I-5 north and US 12 east. Stay on US 12 past Packwood to SR 123, which leads north to the Stevens Canyon Entrance, and across Cayuse Pass (closed in winter) to the White River Entrance.

Fees, Permits, Camping, and Lodging

Entrance Fees

Entrance fees are now collected year-round upon entering the park. You may purchase either a Single Person Entry for $5, which allows entry by foot, bicycle, or motorcycle, or a Single Vehicle Entry for $10. Both are valid for seven days. You can also purchase the Mount Rainier National Park Pass for $20, which is valid for one year from the month of purchase. Another option is to purchase a Golden Eagle Passport for $50, which allows entry to all federal parks or fee areas for one year from the month of purchase. Finally, the Golden Age Passport is available to U.S. residents 62 years old and older and is a lifetime pass valid at all federal fee areas.

Individual Wilderness Permits

Permits are required for all backcountry and wilderness camping year-round and are free of charge. A single Individual Wilderness Permit can be used for up to five persons. Note that permit fees change regularly; contact the park for current information.

Permits may be reserved or obtained on a first-come, first-served basis up to 24 hours before beginning a wilderness hike. Party use limits are in effect for all trailside camps and most cross-country and alpine zones from June 1 through September 30.

Wilderness permits are primarily issued at the following locations:

Summer: Longmire Wilderness Information Center, Jackson Visitor Center at Paradise, White River Wilderness Information Center, and the Wilkeson Ranger Station.

Winter: Longmire Museum and Jackson Visitor Center at Paradise.

Group Wilderness Permits

Mount Rainier has 21 wilderness group sites. For groups of 6 to 12 people, you must obtain a Group Wilderness Permit. Group shelters are available at Indian Bar Camp, Summerland Camp, South Mowich River Camp, and Lake George. The condition of shelters is variable.

The information regarding individual permits is applicable.

Climbing Permits

Anyone planning to hike or climb on glaciers or above Camp Muir and Camp Schurman must obtain a Climbing Permit. The Climbing Permit serves as the Wilderness Permit on trips involving an upper mountain climb only.

Registration with a ranger is required unless otherwise indicated at the registration point. There is a two-people-per-party minimum, and you must be at least 18 years old or have written parental permission. Permits are $15 per person per climb, or $25 annually. Primary permit issue stations are as follows:

Summer: Paradise Ranger Station (next to upper parking lot), White River Wilderness Information Center, and Wilkeson Ranger Station.

Winter: Jackson Visitor Center at Paradise (weekends only) and the Longmire Museum.

Summer and Winter Camping

Summer (June 1 through September 30), and whenever less than 2 feet of snow covers the ground: Group camping is permitted only in group sites at designated trailside camps along the maintained trail system, or on the upper mountain at Camp Muir, Camp Schurman, Camp Hazard, or on snow and ice elsewhere in the alpine zone. In cross-country zones, group camping is not permitted in the summer or when less than 2 feet of snow covers the ground.

There's a Bear Out Here!

As part of a Rainier Mountaineering, Inc. Expedition Seminar, our group was camped at 12,300 feet atop Disappointment Cleaver. This was not an ideal place to camp, because folks were straggling by at all odd hours of the night en route to the summit. It was mid-August and the route was certainly well-traveled.

At about 4:30 A.M. I shuddered awake to the sound of a nasally Boston-type voice. That voice proclaimed, "Theys a beah out heah, theys a beah out heah!" What the heck, was I in the throes of a nightmare? "There's a bear out here!" she was trying to tell us. I yelled back, irritated at the delusions of a tired climber, "And a giraffe too, I bet!"

I stuck my grumpy head out of the tent door and, lo and behold, there was a bear out there! This young adult was gracefully and quickly scampering away from our camp. It must have climbed up the Emmons Glacier for it was already at about 13,000 feet, rapidly heading right up the upper glacier between the top of the cleaver and the

Winter: Group camping is permitted anywhere well away from plowed roads and buildings between October 1 and May 31 when there is at least 2 feet of protective snowcover in the area (5 feet at Paradise) in which you intend to camp. Groups larger than 12 people may camp only in the immediate Paradise area and only within easy walking distance of the rest rooms, located in the upper parking lot, which are open year-round.

Wilderness Camping Options

Trailside, cross-country, and alpine are your three options for camping zones.

Trailside camping: Most camps have toilet facilities, marked sites, and a nearby water source. Camping along trails is permitted only at established trailside camps.

Cross-country camping: Within established cross-country zones you can choose your own campsite. All cross-country sites must be at least ¼ mile away from any road or established trail. Camps must also be at least 100 feet from lakes, streams, and other wetlands.

Cross-country use limits pertain between June 1 and September 30, and whenever less than 2 feet of protective snowcover exists. Cross-country parties may not exceed five people, unless the party is a single immediate family (parents and children).

Between October 1 and May 31 when snow depth is 2 feet or more, cross-country parties may include up to 12 people. At Paradise only, party size is unlimited when the snow is at least 5 feet deep, but parties of more than 12 people must camp within easy walking distance of the 24-hour rest rooms located in the upper parking lot.

Alpine camping: Alpine zones are areas above treeline, generally above 6,000 feet, or elsewhere on exposed rock, glaciers, and snowfields.

Camping is permitted only on permanent snow or ice or on bare ground areas previously used as a campsite. Do not clear tent sites on rocky or snowfree areas. No bare ground camping is permitted below Camp Muir. Group size is limited to 12 for camping on snow and ice, and 5 for bare ground areas.

Anyone intending to travel on glaciers or climb above the normal high camps of Camp Muir or Camp Schurman must purchase a climbing permit.

Reservations for Wilderness and Climbing Permits

Reservations are optional and apply only to the June 1 through September 30 summer season. They are not issued nor needed during the rest of the year.

Up to 60 percent of spaces in trailside camps, cross-country and alpine zones, and at the high-climbing camps are reservable. Permits for the remaining 40 percent are issued on a first-come, first-served basis in the park only on the day the hike or climb begins, or up to 24 hours in advance.

Reservations cost $20 per party (non-refundable) for one continuous backpacking trip or climb. This fee is in addition to the afforementioned climbing permit fees(s). One re-reservation before the start of a trip and one during a trip are permitted without additional charges, both of which depend on remaining space available.

Reservations may be requested up to 60 days before the start of a backpacking trip or climb by phoning the Reservations Office at (360) 569-3317, or in person at the Reservations Office at the Longmire Wilderness Information Center.

Campgrounds

Campgrounds at Ohanapecosh and Cougar Rock are available by reservation only from July 1 through Labor Day. The fee is $14 per site per night. To reserve a site at either campground, contact the National Park Reservation Service (operated by Biospherics, Inc.) up to three months prior to the date you wish to reserve, at (800) 365-2267 (call at least 24 hours in advance, 7:00 A.M. to 7:00 P.M., Pacific Standard Time). Reservation terminals are also located at both these campgrounds. Ohanapecosh is located 11 miles north of Packwood on SR 123 (at the southeast corner of the park). There are 205 campsites. Cougar Rock is located 2½ miles above Longmire on the road to Paradise. There are 5 group sites and 200 individual sites (including 60 pull-through sites for vehicles). Both campgrounds are available on a first-come, first-served basis before July 1 and after Labor Day. The fee during that time is $12 per site per night.

Campsites at Sunshine Point, White River, and Mowich Lake (walk-in only; a short 50-yard hike) are available on a first-come, first-served basis only. Sunshine Point is located ¼ mile east of the Nisqually Entrance (at the southwest corner of the park). There are 18 campsites and the camping fee is $10 per night. White River Campground is located 5 miles west of the White River Entrance, off SR 410 (at the northeast corner of the park). There are 117 campsites and the camping fee is $10 per night. Mowich Lake has 30 undesignated, primitive sites only, without nearby water.

Ipsut Creek Campground (at the northwest corner of the park) has 28 individual campsites. Ipsut Creek is currently being treated as a wilderness campground until the flood-damaged access road has been repaired. As of January 1999, the road is closed indefinitely. A backcountry permit is required and is available on a first-come, first-served basis either at the Carbon River Ranger Station or at a temporary station in Wilkeson.

Lodging

For lodging reservations at one of the two hotels located within the park, the National Park Inn (at Longmire, with 25 rooms) or the Paradise Inn (at Paradise, with 126 rooms), call Mount Rainier Guest Services, Inc. (GSI), at (360) 569-2275.

There are several options for lodging near Ashford, close to the Nisqually Entrance of the park. Consider Whittaker's Bunkhouse, owned by famed Mount Rainier guide Lou Whittaker (a tasteful collection of climbing memorabilia can be found in the coffee shop). Another option is Rainier Overland, a motel and restaurant (which serves the heartiest breakfast for miles). Phones: Bunkhouse, (360) 569-2439; Overland, (360) 569-0851.

Emmons' shoulder. Loping up and away, it was more comical than anything else, and we wondered what would bring a four-legged beast to these heights.

As Dee Molenaar mentioned in his book, The Challenge of Rainier, *Curtis Fawley and crew saw the animal later that morning working its way through the crevasses of the Kautz route. What a sight to have seen! I wonder if the bear summited?*

Alex Van Steen

Supply Availability

Enumclaw and Puyallup have full services available at all times; other towns near the park are more limited. If you're arriving via airplane and need last-minute outdoor supplies, your easiest access to a climbing shop on the way to the mountain will be the Recreational Equipment, Inc. (REI) store in Federal Way, just 15 minutes south of the airport on I-5. Take I-5 exit 143, turn west on 320th, and find REI at the north end of the very first shopping complex on the right-hand side. Other climbing stores in the Seattle area include REI (Seattle), Feathered Friends (across the street from REI in Seattle), Marmot Mountain Supply and Wilderness Sports (Bellevue), and Backpacker's Supply (Tacoma). Near the Nisqually Entrance to the park, the Summit Haus in Ashford offers equipment to rent or purchase.

Climbing Conduct

1. Stay current with issues and regulations. Contact park headquarters at Tahoma Woods with questions (phone (360) 569-2211), or access the National Park Service Mount Rainier website at http://www.nps.gov/mora/
2. Climb in a safe and responsible manner. This goes hand in hand with the suggestions for good climbing practices that follow. Climbers can and have been cited for reckless endangerment for being unsafe on popular routes where their actions threaten the safety of themselves and others around them. Examples include soloing without permission and climbing off-route (thereby bombarding climbers below with loose rock).
3. Adopt good climbing practices. This would include building experience and good judgement by conditioning on easier climbs and participating in mountaineering schools, partaking in rescue, avalanche, and first aid courses, roping up on crevassed terrain, and using appropriate equipment and an appropriate number of team members for the route chosen.
4. Don't count on "pushing your envelope" and ignoring the common-sense rules of conduct only to cry for help later. Rescue helicopters or an army of rescuers are not always available at the touch of a cell phone. Helicopter rescues are extremely dangerous in the mountain environment. Avoid placing yourself (and possibly rescue personnel) in needless peril.
5. Obtain prior written permission from the Superintendent if you intend to climb solo above high camp. Write to: Superintendent, Mount Rainier National Park, Tahoma Woods, Star Route, Ashford, WA 98304. Allow at least two weeks for a response and provide the Superintendent with a supporting resume.
6. Use established trails wherever possible. This is especially important in vegetated areas where a single step can destroy fragile plant life. So often folks "generously" step out of someone else's way only to step off the trail and crush the life out of the meadows. The fragile alpine zones (around 6,000 feet) are particularly sensitive to damaging intrusions. Stay off any

Crevasse rescue practice on the Ingraham Glacier *(Jason Edwards)*

vegetation or bare ground and stick to established trails and snow-protected areas where possible.

7. Please treat the park with respect. Ninety-seven percent of Mount Rainier National Park is designated wilderness. This includes all climbing routes on Mount Rainier.

8. Camp only on permanent snow or ice, or on bare ground areas previously used as campsites. Clearing new tent sites on rocky or snowfree areas is illegal.

9. Don't litter. Pack out all trash; don't crevasse it.

10. Dispose of human waste properly. The toilet facilities provided at Camp Muir and Camp Schurman require that you do not throw garbage or "blue bags" into them. The "blue bags" are available at ranger stations and at the high camps (Camp Muir and Camp Schurman) at no cost to the climber. If you must defecate while climbing, use these "blue bags" to carry human waste off the mountain. "Blue bags" should be deposited in collection barrels at Camp Muir, Camp Schurman, Camp Hazard, Emmons Flats, or Ingraham Flats.

11. Car pool or use the shuttles when possible. This will be particularly helpful in cutting down on parking congestion at Paradise and White River.

Climbing Safety

Alex Van Steen

With more than two hundred attempts on Mount Rainier under my belt this past decade, I feel fortunate to have been involved as a responder in only a dozen or so rescues. Not surprisingly, I have observed practices that have scared the daylights

out of me. Fortunately, people tend to survive their duller moments. Unfortunately, some reckless climbers won't acknowledge the hazard they've become to both themselves and to others. Certainly as climbing grows in popularity, safe climbing practices become even more essential.

Climbing safely is a responsibility that must reach deeper than our desire to reach the summit. To extend ourselves much beyond our limits and risk injury or death is foolhardy, and makes us irresponsible. In 1993 I saw a Denali summiter being evacuated at the 14,000-foot camp to a helicopter waiting nearby. Waving his frostbitten hands from atop his stretcher, he was yelling "Victory! Victory!" I suggest, "Not!!"

Climbing safely begins with a healthy respect for mountains. More people have died near the sloping Muir Snowfield than on the obviously threatening Willis Wall. This is partly because climbers who have reached the Willis Wall usually belong there; they're advanced/skilled climbers using good style and technique, aware of and somewhat prepared to deal with the hazards. Conversely, people without proper equipment or an understanding of the terrain often walk into trouble on the seemingly benign Muir Snowfield.

People have strayed into the Nisqually or Paradise Glacier drainages by error, or spent the night sitting out in clouds (sometimes quite near Paradise), when a compass might have guided them safely down. Even people with some experience regularly attempt to negotiate Rainier's snowfields without proper navigation equipment. Proper equipment and an experience level appropriate to the outing are essential ingredients for success on any mountain. A compass and map and the skill to use them are minimum requirements to be on any mountain. Deaths have occurred for lack of the basics. A healthy respect for the mountains means understanding that difficult climbing can be safe and easy climbing can be dangerous.

A healthy attitude and proper gear are a good start, but the best defense against potential problems is to educate yourself in the way of the mountains. Quality instructional courses in basic mountaineering, wilderness first aid courses, avalanche courses, and mountain rescue courses are all beneficial. And there is no substitute for lots of practice on easier peaks.

Complacency and improper equipment jeopardize the safety of individuals, their teammates, and other parties on the mountain. For example, using lighweight shoes such as sneakers or approach shoes, which are not crampon-compatible, and ski sticks instead of ice axes, is ill advised. When a group stands

John Cumming jumps a crevasse on the Cowlitz Glacier. *(Jason Edwards)*

together with coiled ropes on a crevasse bridge, peering curiously into the abyss, have they thought about the bridge's stability? Is their only gauge the fact that others have already crossed it? Why do some parties crowd behind a slow-moving group, then find themselves held up in a rockfall or icefall hazard area? It would be much better to wait in a safe area while the group ahead clears through the dangers. These are just a few situations where a little education and experience can help.

As a guide on the mountain for the past decade, I have learned the importance of thinking ahead. What would happen if ...? What would happen if my ropemate fell right now? What would happen if that iceblock hanging above us cut loose? Think through the scenarios and have a plan of action if something does happen. It will make your ascent of any mountain a far better adventure.

The Grading System

Grades have been included on all main routes to help climbers objectively evaluate the difficulties of particular routes. The dangers of a route, however, are not as easily categorized. Be aware that all crevassed routes, regardless of grade, require a rope, and even the easiest routes may have significant crevasse, icefall, and avalanche hazard.

I   Relatively easy climbing where the ice axe serves mostly as a point of balance rather than a tool for ascent. There is generally little risk of serious injury. A Grade I climb will require only one or two days to complete.

II   Easy climbing, but with some exposure. A fall could hurt or kill you, but you probably won't fall. Still a one or two day climb.

III Slightly more difficult climbing where hands will be brought in to help not only with balance but with movement as well. Can involve steep faces and exposed ridges. Optimistically a full day's climb, but typically at least an overnighter.

IV   Difficult climbing where a rope is used continuously. These require a night or two on the route, although many have been climbed in a 24–hour period.

V   Very technical climbing that requires the use of protection to shorten the length of possible falls. At least two nights are usually needed for these climbs. Routes graded V on Mount Rainier usually involve exposure to significant objective hazard.

Maps

Relevant USGS topographic maps covering the mountain are Mount Rainier East, Mount Rainier West, Mowich Lake, Sunrise. All are at a 1:24,000 scale. Several other maps are also available.

For More Information

To contact a climbing ranger for updated information on weather, route conditions, crevasses, rock fall, and avalanches, or to contact park headquarters for Mount Rainier National Park, write Tahoma Woods, Star Route, Ashford, WA 98304-9751; or call (360) 569-2211.

Current weather information can be accessed on the World Wide Web at http://www.intellicast.com/weather/sea/ or http://www.wrh.noaa.gov/

For avalanche conditions, call the Northwest Weather and Avalanche Center at (206) 526-6677 (Washington and northern Oregon), or (503) 808-2400 (Washington's southern Cascades and Oregon).

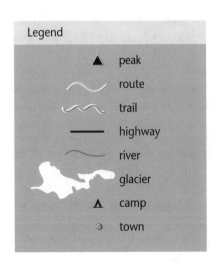

Legend

▲ peak

route

trail

highway

river

glacier

▲ camp

○ town

A party traverses the scary "bowling alley," notorious for rockfall and exposure. This is not a place to get trapped behind a slower party! (*Jason Edwards*)

Ingraham and Nisqually Glaciers

When looking up at Mount Rainier from the south, the spectacular Nisqually Glacier overwhelms the view. The Nisqually Glacier extends from the crater rim for 3¾ miles into its deep canyon west of Paradise Park, ending near the altitude of 4,800 feet. It is one of six glaciers on the mountain that originate on the summit dome and extend completely to the river valleys at its foot. Together with its tributary, the Wilson Glacier, the Nisqually system has an area of some 2.2 square miles. The standard approach for all the Nisqually routes is to climb the Muir Snowfield to Camp Muir (see description for Disappointment Cleaver approach), although many variations exist and an ascent of the complete Nisqually Glacier from its toe has been documented.

The Ingraham Glacier, a major feature of both the Disappointment Cleaver and Ingraham Glacier routes, is a long, narrow ice stream on Mount Rainier's southeast flank, joining the Cowlitz Glacier just below Cathedral Rocks Ridge at 6,800 feet. On the south the glacier is bounded by Gibraltar Rock and Cathedral Rocks, and on the north by Little Tahoma and Disappointment Cleaver; this cleaver separates the Ingraham from the Emmons Glacier. Between 7,000 feet and 9,000 feet the Ingraham makes its steepest gradient, forming an icefall (this lower Ingraham Icefall does not affect climbing parties).

The Ingraham flows from the summit dome, while the Cowlitz (its southerly branch) heads a cirque immediately beneath Gibraltar Rock. The lower ice stream of the Ingraham ends at about 5,500 feet, in a steep-walled canyon, here bordered by long morainal ridges.

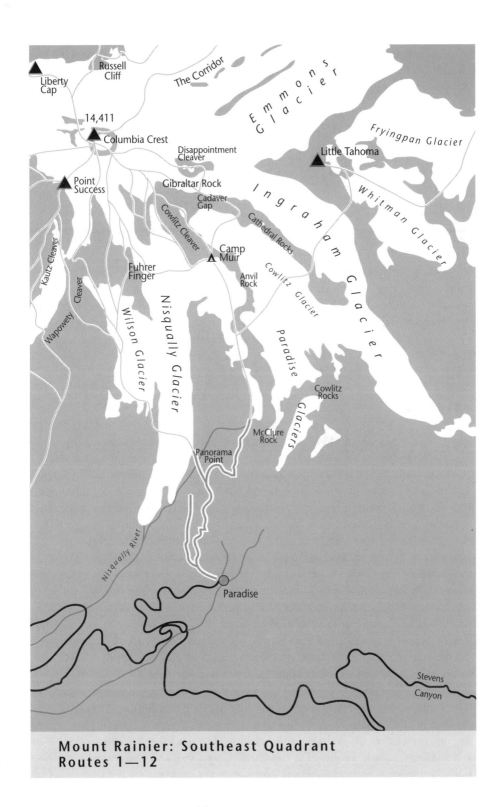

Liberty
Cap

Russell
Cliff

The Corridor

E m m o n s
G l a c i e r

Fryingpan Glacier

14,411

Columbia Crest

Disappointment
Cleaver

Little Tahoma

Whitman Glacier

Point
Success

Gibraltar Rock

Cadaver
Gap

I n g r a h a m   G l a c i e r

Kautz Cleaver

Cowlitz Cleaver

Cathedral Rocks

Camp
Muir

Fuhrer
Finger

Anvil
Rock

Cowlitz Glacier

Cleaver

Wapowety

Wilson Glacier

N i s q u a l l y   G l a c i e r

P a r a d i s e

Cowlitz
Rocks

McClure
Rock

G l a c i e r s

Panorama
Point

Nisqually River

Paradise

Stevens

Canyon

**Mount Rainier: Southeast Quadrant
Routes 1—12**

In September 1885 (possibly 1886), Allison L. Brown and a party of Yakima Indians climbed the glacier to an unknown height. It is not certain just who made the first complete ascent of the glacier.

1. Disappointment Cleaver

This route, which combines the Cowlitz Glacier, Cathedral Rocks Ridge, the Ingraham Glacier, and Disappointment Cleaver, has become by far the most popular on Mount Rainier. Approximately two-thirds of the climbers attempting Mount Rainier use this route. The Cleaver portion of the route (11,200 feet to 12,400 feet) is usually only done in mid- and late-summer after its steepness has melted off, and after the central and upper sections of the Ingraham Glacier become quite broken. The upper glacier's condition changes from year to year.

During good weather in the summer season, this route and its variations are exceedingly popular. The advantage for the climber here is a well-marked track (usually "kicked in" by the guide service) and the "security" of others nearby. The disadvantage is overcrowding on the route and the diminishment of the "wilderness" experience. Camping quotas at Camp Muir and Ingraham Flats to some extent govern the number of persons on the route. These quotas are revised as the National Park Service continues to evaluate its policies and procedures.

Procedure

Nearly all parties begin at Paradise (5,420 feet) and hike the western loop of the Skyline Trail via Alta Vista (½ mile), Glacier Vista (1⅕ miles), and Panorama Point (2 ½ miles; 6,800 feet). At this point, one is above and east of the Nisqually Glacier. The route and tread (often snow-covered) continues to Pebble Creek (7,200 feet). Here the Muir Snowfield begins. Moon Rocks (9,200 feet) is an important navigation landmark and is situated prominently along the route. The entire trip up to the Muir Snowfield is about 4½ miles, and ends at Camp Muir (10,062 feet).

Beware of hiking or skiing onto the steep Nisqually Glacier slope to the west, or the Paradise and Cowlitz Glacier flanks to the east in poor visibility. There are steep cliffs east of McClure Rock (site of Mount Rainier's first fatality when, in 1897, Edgar McClure tripped and slid down into the Paradise Glacier basin to his death) and to the east from Anvil Rock to Camp Muir. Be aware that Panorama Point has a steep west-facing slope that is prone to avalanche in winter and spring.

If visibility is poor, the following compass readings may be useful: Pebble Creek to Moon Rocks—350 degrees true north and 328 degrees magnetic north; the reverse reading is 170 degrees true north and 148 degrees magnetic north. Moon Rocks to Camp Muir—344 degrees true north and 322 degrees magnetic north; the reverse reading is 164 degrees true north and 142 degrees magnetic north. Time: Allow four to seven hours to reach Camp Muir, where there are toilet facilities. The shelter and tenting space is set up on a quota basis, and you will know your allocation upon receiving a permit. Climbers commonly set up tents in the snow nearby,

Nisqually Icecliff and Gibraltar Rock *(Jim Stuart)*

Disappointment Cleaver

Gibraltar Rock

Ingraham Glacier

eyebolt

Gibraltar Ledge

Nisqually-Gibraltar Chute

Nisqually Icecliff

Nisqually Cleaver

American Lung Association climbers head away from the top of Disappointment Cleaver (12,400 feet) toward the Ingraham Headwall. *(Barry Gregg)*

generally on either side of the ridge where winds are less severe. Do not camp near the guide service water system (large barrels and siphon hoses). Camping on the helicopter landing pad (near the public latrines) is also not recommended.

In the summer season there is a park ranger (with radio) stationed at Camp Muir. In winter, all the shelters may be closed by snow but can normally be dug out if you bring a shovel. The public facilities are on the east (right) end of the ridge while Rainier Mountaineering and the National Park Service facilities dominate the west (left) side of the ridge. There is an emergency radio in the public stone shelter in winter.

From Camp Muir, gain access to the Ingraham Glacier by a nearly level traverse of the upper Cowlitz Glacier and ascend the slope through 10,500-foot Higher Cathedral Gap (the central of three gaps in Cathedral Rocks Ridge). At the gap climb a snow, or long scree, slope to the crest (with some exposure to rockfall from the left), then set onto the Ingraham. You soon reach Ingraham Flats (11,000 feet), a very popular camping area. Make a glacier traverse between about 11,000 and 11,200 feet (depending on crevasses) to the low southern base of Disappointment Cleaver. Most parties leave the glacier about 200 to 300 feet above the cleaver's base to begin the ascent.

A ledge system (three possible access ledges exist) of loose rock provides access to the cleaver crest snowfield. Climb to the top of the cleaver, then continue toward the east crater rim. The route on the upper mountain will be affected by existing crevasses. In middle or late season it is usually more prudent to bear toward the Emmons Glacier, where there are fewer crevasses at this level, although in many years it is possible to climb directly above Disappointment Cleaver toward the summit dome.

The east crater is a circular rock-rimmed depression filled with snow and marked by steam fumaroles. Columbia Crest, at 14,411.1 feet, is the true summit, and is located on the western rim. The summit register is at a three-rock outcrop on the inside of, and about 300 linear feet from, the crater's north–northeast rim. The western crater is southwest of Columbia Crest.

Warnings and suggestions: There tends to be late-season rockfall danger on the cleaver, and while some of it is generated spontaneously, it most often is the result of the carelessness of climbers. Be especially careful not to scramble off the beaten path, a sometimes difficult task in the darkness of the early morning. Courteous and safe climbers attempt to move through areas of loose rock only when others are not below them.

It is also important not to linger in rockfall areas. The most critical area on this route is between "The Icebox," that heavily crevassed portion of the Ingraham Glacier just west of the cleaver, and the true spine of the cleaver. Avoiding bottlenecks here or at any hazardous spot on the route is vital. A party that is stopped and blocking the route may cause others to wait in a precarious position. If you are stopping to rest (even momentarily), get off the route so others can pass.

Grade I or II; bring snow anchors such as pickets and crevasse extrication equipment. Time: Five to eight hours from Camp Muir to the crater rim.

Ascent variation via Cadaver Gap: From Camp Muir, ascend the Cowlitz Glacier diagonally to a moderately steep snow chute on Cathedral Rocks Ridge. This leads to

Morning sun warms climbers as they approach Ingraham Flats at 11,000 feet on the Ingraham Glacier. This is traditionally the first good rest break, about one hour into the climb. (*Alex Van Steen*)

11,300-foot Cadaver Gap, between the ridge and Gibraltar Rock. Now cross through to the Ingraham Glacier, then either climb the headwall (the direct route), staying close to Gibraltar, or cross to Disappointment Cleaver. It also should be noted that this portion of the route is most free of crevasses and safest in early season, but is exposed to rockfall from the face of Gibraltar. A fatal slab avalanche occurred on this route in March 1979 below Cadaver Gap. This route is not advised (or possible) in late season due to rockfall and crevasses.

Ascent variation, Ingraham and Emmons Glaciers (traverse below Disappointment Cleaver): It is possible to avoid the crowds on Disappointment Cleaver by dropping off of Ingraham Flats at 11,000 feet to access the large basin at the base of the cleaver. A great campsite exists here, as long as one moves far enough east to be free of any icefall hazard. The altitude drop of 500 feet is rewarded by the isolation gained, but presents a somewhat punishing uphill section if one uses the same route to return.

From this basin it is possible to access either the eastern slopes of the cleaver, which can be climbed back up to the standard route (usually only an early season option, due to the bergschrund

First Attempt on Rainier

Lt. August Valentine Kautz became important in Mount Rainier history when, in August 1857, he made the first serious climb on the mountain. It is likely he would have made the first ascent but for an underestimation of the length of the climb and the fatigue of his companions.

A German immigrant, Kautz was a West Point classmate of John Mullan and George Crook, both future Pacific Northwest explorers (Crook, when a general, became the West's most famous Indian fighter).

Kautz served with distinction in the Indian and Civil wars and later became a brigadier general. While leading a charge against hostile Indians at the White River in 1856, Kautz was wounded in the leg, but in one month he was able to lead a scouting detachment to Mount Rainier's foothills. He became familiar with the Indian trail to the Nisqually River, and during his garrison duty at Fort Steilacoom, the sight of Mount Rainier stirred his interest to make a summit attempt.

that opens up dramatically in late season), or continue up the Emmons Glacier toward the top of the cleaver (usually gaining the standard route at the 12,600-foot level).

Approach variation: The access to the lower Cowlitz and Ingraham Glaciers is easily done by crossing the small Paradise and Williwakus Glaciers just south of Cowlitz Rocks. Drop off the Cowlitz Divide to access one of two routes to the Cowlitz Glacier below. The descent routes avoid the steep cliffs directly below, one at each end of the band. Good campsites abound, on both the Cowlitz Divide and the Cowlitz Glacier.

Climb the Cowlitz Glacier on its left side, thus avoiding the serious lower Cowlitz and Ingraham icefalls at the confluence of those glaciers. Choose to negotiate either the upper Paradise Glacier or remain on the Cowlitz Glacier (as crevasses dictate; the farther west, or left, the simpler it usually is to gain the upper Cowlitz area). Note that this is usually only a good variation in early season.

2. Ingraham Glacier

The upper Ingraham Glacier is an early season route, usually climbed from above Ingraham Flats through its center to the top of Disappointment Cleaver.

Follow the route directions for Disappointment Cleaver access (from Camp Muir or an access variation). One can wait until reaching the area of Ingraham Flats before making the decision regarding taking the Ingraham or bearing rightward to the Cleaver. In midseason either option makes sense; in late season the Cleaver is recommended. Also, the number of parties and crowding on the Cleaver can affect the decision.

The upper Ingraham climb normally begins near its center above Ingraham Flats, or just right of center, as the crevasses dictate. It then joins the Cleaver route from 12,200 feet to 12,600 feet, just as it steepens. Sometimes a good portion of these two routes may overlap, especially in early season under abundant snowcover.

Grade I or II; bring pickets and crevasse rescue equipment. Time: Five to seven hours from Camp Muir (nine to eleven hours round trip).

Ascent variation, west along upper Gibraltar Rock: A very early season variation (with ample snow) is to skirt Gibraltar Rock, then bear toward the Nisqually Glacier. An alternate is to head back above the Cleaver.

Ascent variation, climbing the Headwall directly: Another variation is to climb the Ingraham directly from the Flats to the summit, through the Headwall. This has been done occasionally in early summer when the snowcover was quite thick.

3. Gibraltar Ledge, Post-1948 Route

Gibraltar, the gigantic wedge-shaped formation on the southeast flank of Mount Rainier, whose peak is 12,660 feet in altitude, is composed of south-dipping interlayered lava, tuff, breccia, and pumice, with a thick and shattered andesite base. As a climbing route to the summit, Gibraltar remained the normal way from the first ascent of the mountain in 1870 until well into the twentieth century. The slanting ledges on the west face of the rock fell into disfavor because of a steep snow traverse and objective dangers from rockfall. In 1936 a section of the route fell away, closing the route for some years until a lower ledge bypass was found. As a route, it is certainly direct; it is climbed most often in winter and spring, the safest period for this route. The first ascent of the mountain, by Hazard Stevens and Philemon Van Trump in August 1870, and the second ascent, by Allen Wilson and Samuel Emmons in October of that year, were made by this route.

Procedure

Follow the directions for the Disappointment Cleaver and Ingraham Glacier routes to Camp Muir. Climb diagonally to the head of the Cowlitz Glacier at 11,500 feet, passing beneath a landmark tower on the ridge (The Beehive). Cross Cowlitz Cleaver at a high notch to reach the Gibraltar Ledge.

Variations exist when avalanche hazard or open crevasses force an ascent that more directly follows the Cowlitz Cleaver ridge. After skirting the west side of The Beehive, a short drop-off or rappel will gain the Cowlitz Glacier. Climbers often fix a section

An RMI client paying close attention while crossing a ladder that spans a deep crevasse at the base of the steepening Ingraham Glacier. He furtively exits an area known as "The Icebox." (*Alex Van Steen*)

(25 feet) of rope here to facilitate their return. In some years this is just a step off the ridge and onto the snow.

Then follow snow (or steep scree later in the season) on the rock's west face. (Note: An eye bolt was placed to make a rappel, and traditionally has been recommended as a lowering point. However, it is no longer necessary to go up to this bolt. A simple traverse across steep snow or scree exists about 50 feet below it.)

Now follow the ledge below the cliff of Gibraltar's southwest face, above the narrowing that drops into the Nisqually amphitheater, to a narrow stance just east of a prominent ice chute. Proceed to the ice chute (the Nisqually–Gibraltar Chute)

on the left, which becomes the most technical portion of the route. Ascend this chute nearly to the upper end of Gibraltar, and go on to the saddle at its top. Now ascend moderate glacier slopes (the Nisqually Glacier) directly to the eastern crater rim.

Climbers traversing Gibraltar Ledge *(Jeff Chichester)*

The compass bearing from the saddle to the rim is 310 degrees true north. In early season few crevasses appear, but they may become more of a route problem after the month of June. Early season climbers will want to have a sound understanding of avalanche awareness and not be lured by the tradition of this route.

Grades I and II. Time: Four to eight hours from Camp Muir.

4. Nisqually–Gibraltar Chute, 1946

This thin chute separates the Nisqually Glacier from Gibraltar Rock. Receding as the summer season progresses, icefall from the overhanging Nisqually Icecliff and rockfall from Gibraltar's west face continually bombard and scar this gully. Additionally, Nisqually Icecliff colapses can often be seen from far down the Muir Snowfield, dramatically blasting its length with wind and debris.

This route was first done by ski racer Paul Gilbreath, Stan de Bruler, and a person named Hewitt (July 1946).

Opposite: A party drops off of the upper Nisqually Glacier onto the ledge of Gibraltar during a March 1998 climb. *(Len Kannapell)*

View of the normally dangerous chute in particularly hazardous conditions. *(Alex Van Steen)*

Procedure

This route traverses around the western base of Cowlitz Cleaver onto the Nisqually Glacier, then to the base of Gibraltar. To avoid crevasses in this portion of the route, keep on the west base of the cleaver.

Now climb directly up the steep snow-ice chute between the Nisqually Icecliff and Gibraltar to join the Gibraltar Ledge route at the level of the main ledge. This is

Opposite: Mount Rainier from the east *(Bob and Ira Spring)*

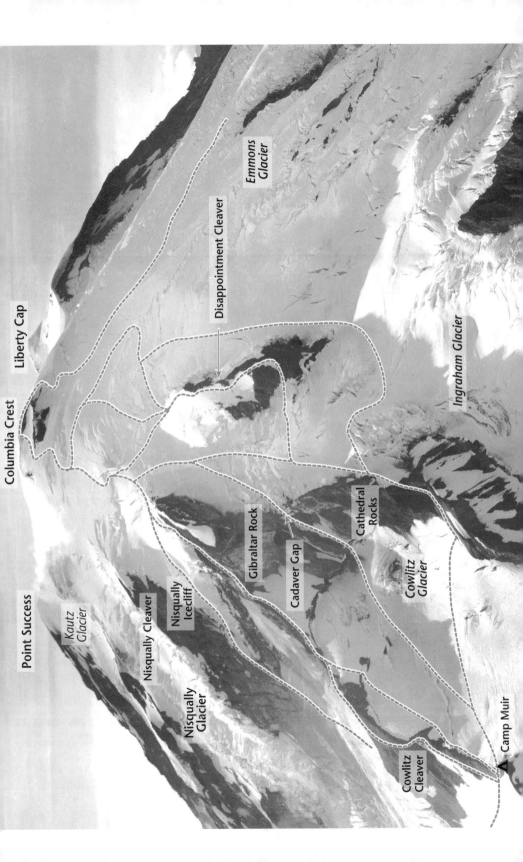

Columbia Crest

Liberty Cap

Point Success

Kautz Glacier

Nisqually Cleaver

Nisqually Icecliff

Nisqually Glacier

Gibraltar Rock

Cadaver Gap

Cathedral Rocks

Cowlitz Glacier

Cowlitz Cleaver

Camp Muir

Disappointment Cleaver

Emmons Glacier

Ingraham Glacier

Tom Stewart and Al Errington ascend the Nisqually Icecliff during a winter ascent. *(Stewart Collection, photographer unknown)*

best done in early season and under cold conditions to avoid objective danger. Grade III. Time: Four to six hours from Camp Muir.

5. Nisqually Icecliff, 1962

There is a prominent, 200-foot icecliff that terminates at the eastern lobe of the upper Nisqually Glacier. At its lower western extremity, the icecliff narrows to a point, where it may be climbed from the amphitheater below. However, changing ice conditions or lateness of season when snow in the glacial amphitheater is low may render the route hazardous or unfeasible. The first ascent was made by Barry Bishop and Luther Jerstad (of Mount Everest fame) on August 13, 1962. The first winter climb was done by Eric Simonson and Jerry Hasfjord on March 3 and 4, 1975.

Procedure

Make the approach as for the Nisqually–Gibraltar Chute. Be aware of objective hazards and plan accordingly. The chute leading to the lower left point of the cliff is the steepest portion. Grade III. Time: Six hours from Camp Muir.

6. Nisqually Icefall, 1948

The icefall of the upper Nisqually Glacier, visible from afar, is the most impressive and chaotic on Mount Rainier's southern flank. The Nisqually Glacier near 13,000 feet is split by the Nisqually Cleaver, a prominent rock buttress. The eastern glacier lobe descends west of Gibraltar Rock to form an icecliff at about 12,000 feet. Avalanches from the icecliff fall into the large cirque below the Gibraltar level. The Nisqually Icefall originates from the western lobe of the glacier, forming a narrow and constantly changing ice cascade between Wapowety Cleaver (on the west)

Climbers thread the maze of crevasses on their approach to the Nisqually Icefall *(Jason Edwards)*

Nisqually Cleaver— A One-Day Attempt

In April 1983, Craig Van Hoy and I planned to climb the Nisqually Cleaver from Paradise in a day. We started out late one Friday evening, then left Camp Muir at 4:00 A.M. in the cold dark. We made quick progress up the 30- to 50-degree slopes. Our route took us directly above the entrance chute, through several rock bands, and across hanging snowfields. The conditions were reasonable, but occasional deep snow required two tools used in the "cane" position to make upward progress. A few running belays were placed along the way, and we reached the summit at 10:00 A.M. in a raging blizzard. After a few minutes' rest we descended via the Ingraham Glacier and promptly got lost in the storm. We were thoroughly exhausted when we finally reached Muir after nine hours of struggling through the raging weather. So much for our one-day climb!

Jason Edwards

and Nisqually Cleaver (on the east). The steepest portion of the icefall is between 10,500 and 12,500 feet.

As a climb, the route can be an enigma. Glacier movement and the season will dictate the character of the icefall section of the Nisqually. Due to crevasse openings and sérac instability, the adventurous climber is wise to undertake the ascent during late spring or early summer, during low temperatures. Certainly the ascent is unwise after mid-July. In any event, there is a certain risk, although some parties have found the climb quite safe. Be aware that séracs can tumble, and that there can be hazards from falling débris. The first ascent was made by veteran Mount Rainier climber and author Dee Molenaar and Robert W. Craig on July 15, 1948.

Procedure

From Camp Muir, make a westerly traverse (beneath Cowlitz Cleaver) and cross the crevasse and sérac patterns. Large holes above the main icefall can be a problem, but once above 12,500 feet the slope eases and smoothes out. Head for the crater rim. Grade III or IV. Time: Six to ten hours from Camp Muir.

7. Nisqually Cleaver, 1967

This climb, first done by Fred Dunham and Jim Wickwire on June 19, 1967, ascends the upper portion of the cleaver; overall, the cleaver extends from 10,600 feet to 13,000 feet.

Procedure

From the base of the Cowlitz Cleaver, traverse left beneath the precarious Nisqually Icecliff to the narrow chute that is the starting point for both the Nisqually Cleaver and Nisqually Icecliff routes. This steep chute accesses the sweeping slopes of the flanks of the Nisqually Cleaver that climb to the crest of the ridge at roughly 50 degrees. While the route bypasses the large rotten rock step that is the actual toe of the ridge, it is much safer since the rock step and the true cleaver crest are almost continuously bombarded by collapses of the Nisqually Icefall's séracs hanging above it. From the chute, continue upward, either directly through the series of small rock bands or occasionally veering right toward the Nisqually Icecliff to avoid some difficulties. Ascending to the cleaver's termination ends the more technically difficult section of the route, and once the moats separating the cleaver from the Nisqually Glacier are crossed, the route joins the Gibraltar Ledge finish to the crater rim. This route, as much or more than any other in its grade, is an intimidating and exposed adventure.

Grade III or IV; bring pickets, ice screws, and possibly some rock protection. Time: Six to eight hours from Camp Muir.

Opposite: Mount Rainier from the southwest *(Jim Stuart)*

Columbia Crest

Point Success

Liberty Cap

Sunset Ridge

Kautz Headwall

Wilson Headwall

ice-cliff

Fuhrer Finger

Camp Hazard

Wapowety Cleaver

The Turtle

Kautz Glacier

Kautz Cleaver

Sunset Amphitheater

11,700' gendarme

red tower

Tahoma Cleaver

Success Cleaver

Success Glacier

Pyramid Glacier

An unusual camp at the very base of Fuhrer Finger, photographed from the edge of the Wilson Glacier *(Jason Edwards)*

8. Fuhrer Finger, 1920

This feature of Mount Rainier is a narrow couloir that slants upward from the head of the Wilson Glacier (at about 10,000 feet) to access gentler upper slopes at 11,500 feet on the western edge of the upper Nisqually Glacier. The first ascent of this route was made by the guides Hans and Heinie Fuhrer (hence the name), Joseph Hazard, Peyton Farrer, and Thomas Hermans on July 2, 1920. While this route may actually be the shortest one to the mountain's summit, it is not necessarily the fastest. While there is no large campsite area, the route is seldom crowded. It is best for a small, moderately fast, and competent party, and should be done before mid-July to avoid the problem of crevasses opening on the upper Nisqually.

Rockfall should be anticipated. Climbing the route during the cold of the morning, and climbing it quickly, eliminates most exposure to rockfall.

Procedure

See directions to access the Kautz Glacier route. Descend the Nisqually Moraine Trail to the lower Nisqually and cross it near the 6,200-foot level. Ascend the Wilson Gully on the west side of the glacier, then ascend the Wilson to about 9,000 feet. Cross the glacier diagonally upward and rightward toward the base of the rock cleaver separating the Wilson and Nisqually Glaciers. A high camp can be made at around 9,500 feet on the cleaver. Time: Six hours to here.

Now, do not waste time with a breakfast that you will not enjoy anyway. Get moving early and get up the route before the sun hits it. Once the sun strikes the

Two climbers
progressing in the upper
couloir of the Finger at
11,000 feet
(Tom Stewart)

rocks high above the gully, stones can begin raining down into the lower gully, where the unaware climber, still in the shade, is endangered. One could keep to the left side of the upper gully to avoid possible rockfall. This is about 5 degrees steeper (about 45 degrees), but safer. The crux of the route, especially as the season progresses, may be getting out of the couloir and onto the Nisqually. It may be necessary to travel west onto the upper Wilson Headwall for a short distance. From the top of Wapowety Cleaver (13,000 feet) move around the crevasses as necessary and head for the crater rim.

Grade II. Time: Five to seven hours from high camp.

Keep in mind the rockfall danger is greatest when the sun is on the route during descent. Avoid glissading the couloir; this could be very dangerous. Several climbers have injured themselves (some seriously) when glissading with crampons on, or when losing control of their glissade.

9. Fuhrer Thumb, 1972

The two spur couloirs of Fuhrer Thumb rise for about 1,500 feet just west of Fuhrer Finger and have been climbed via two lines. The lower, main route, which stays to the right while maintaining an angle similar to Fuhrer Finger (40 degrees), may be more aesthetic due to the confinement by the binding rock walls. For this reason, and the fact that the snow slopes of the gully tend to closely follow the fall line, a helmet and sharp lookout must be used to protect against rock fall. First ascent by Jim Wickwire, Charlie Raymond, and Tom Stewart on May 27, 1972.

The upper route, a minor ascent variation first climbed by Neils Anderson and party on May 28, 1972, is best climbed early season, when the steep, obvious gully through the rock island is snow filled. Grade II. Time: Five to seven hours from high camp.

An RMI Expedition Seminar moves through the lower Wilson Glacier *(Joe Stermitz)*

10. Wilson Headwall, 1957

Dramatic sun-cupped snow pinnacles provide security for Dan Davis and Bruce Laughlin as they high-step up the Wilson Headwall. *(Tom Stewart)*

First ascent of the Wilson Headwall was by Dee Molenaar and Pete Schoening on July 21, 1957.

After crossing the bergschrund at the head of the Wilson Glacier, traverse left into the central snow couloir. Staying left in this couloir may be your best defense against falling rock. A short band of rock must be climbed to access the broad central snow slopes above. Another rock band must be passed above 12,000 feet before cresting on upper Wapowety Cleaver and the upper Nisqually Glacier. Grade II or III. Time: Five to seven hours from high camp.

Ascent variation (minor), 1967 route left of rock island: A variation was made on August 6, 1967 by Dan Davis, Tom Stewart, and Bruce Loughlin. This party climbed from the bergschrund traverse left past the first couloir and ascended snow slopes of the left flank of a prominent rock island in the center of the headwall. They continued to a notch at the top of the island. The climb ascended up the snow until it was possible to traverse rightward to the slopes above the main cliff band, finally joining the original route at the central snow and ice slope.

Both of the upper small rock bands were passed on the right. The 1967 party made a bivouac at 10,000 feet on a rock shoulder to the right of the headwall gully. Grade II or III. Time: Five to seven hours from high camp.

Jim Hamilton climbs the beautiful red andesite on the Wilson Headwall. *(Jason Edwards)*

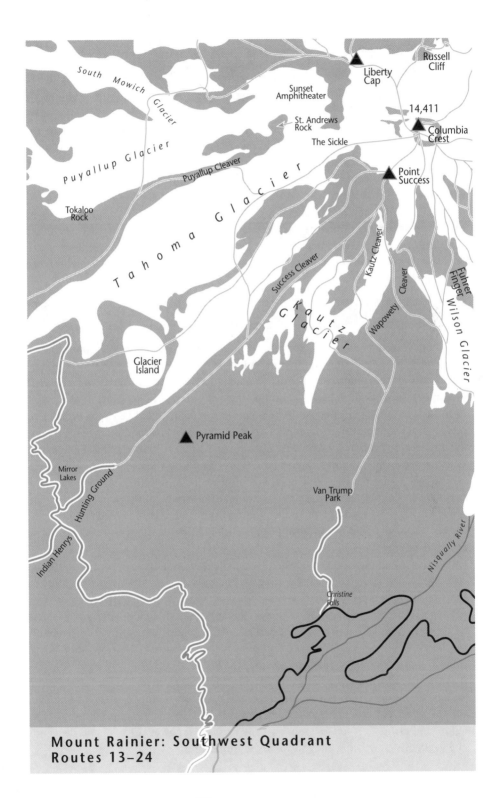

South Mowich Glacier

Puyallup Glacier

Puyallup Cleaver

Tokaloo Rock

Sunset Amphitheater

St. Andrews Rock

The Sickle

Liberty Cap

Russell Cliff

14,411

Columbia Crest

Point Success

Tahoma Glacier

Success Cleaver

Kautz Cleaver

Kautz Glacier

Wapowety Cleaver

Fuhrer Finger

Wilson Glacier

Glacier Island

Pyramid Peak

Mirror Lakes

Hunting Ground

Indian Henrys

Van Trump Park

Nisqually River

Christine Falls

Mount Rainier: Southwest Quadrant
Routes 13–24

Southern and Western Flanks

Covering nearly one-half of Mount Rainier's sprawling circumference, the broad southern and western flanks present a commanding vista from the forested Puget Sound Lowland. With the Nisqually Valley as the most practical access to the mountain, early explorers and mountaineers entered by this approach to attempt the mountain and make discoveries.

A great rock cleaver, the Success, dominates the southwest flank of the volcano, while two grand glaciers, the Kautz and Tahoma, emanate from the icy summit dome. There has been vast glacial recession in the past century, but the actively cascading Tahoma continues to carve a deep gash into the upper cliffs. The shrinking Puyallup Glacier extended nearly to the valley floor in the early nineteenth century. Surprisingly, some of the most recent technical climbing routes were accomplished on this western flank.

11. Kautz Glacier, 1920

The Kautz Glacier was named for Lt. Augustine Valentine Kautz, who first climbed it and made his heroic summit attempt on July 15, 1857. Lt. Kautz, a stalwart German-born army officer stationed at Fort Steilacoom, likely would have succeeded in attaining Mount Rainier's highest point had he not grossly underestimated the length of the ascent and had he been outfitted with warmer clothing. The young pioneering officer, wearing homemade "creepers" (crampons) on his leather boots and carrying an alpenstock, probably reached an altitude of 13,000 feet after climbing a glacier later named in his honor. It was merely a névé hike to the crater rim, but Kautz, aware that to be caught high on the mountain at nightfall could be fatal, and concerned about his several straggling companions, reluctantly gave up his gallant bid. The inexperienced but audacious Kautz, led through the lowland forest by the Indian Wapowety, had found a route to the mountain's glaciers and proved that it could be climbed.

It was well into the next century before Kautz's route was completed. The route was ascended to the crater rim (using a direct ascent over the icecliff) on July 28, 1920 by the Swiss guides Hans and Heinie Fuhrer, leading Roger W. Toll and Harry M. Myers.

Four years later, in 1924, mountaineer Joseph Hazard led an exploratory ascent along the route to assess Kautz's earlier achievement, concluding he probably reached the summit icecap region. Camp Hazard, at about 11,200 feet and the usual camp for climbers using this route, is named for him.

The south-southwest–facing Kautz Glacier emanates from Mount Rainier's summit icecap, then pours through a narrow constriction between two cleavers before it widens again and continues as a slope and valley glacier to a canyon terminus well below timberline. It is located immediately west of Wapowety Cleaver and descends in a gradually narrowing canyon to below timberline.

Opposite: Mount Rainier from the southwest (*Jim Stuart*)

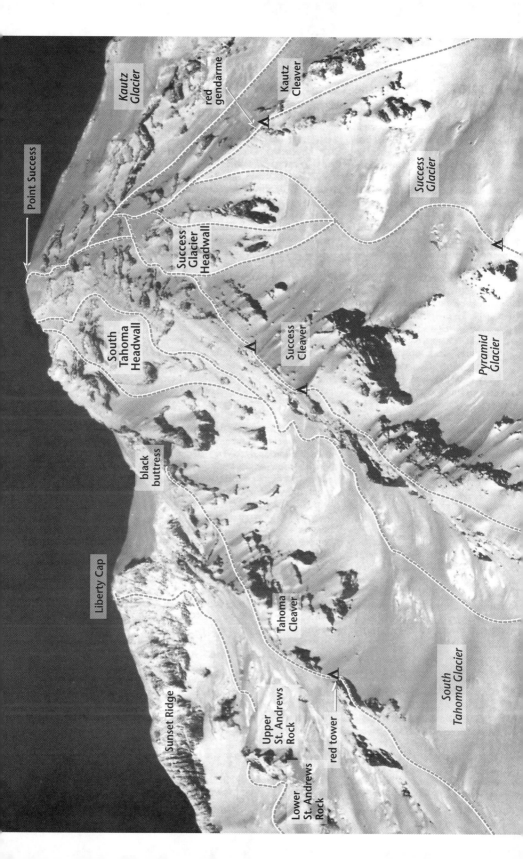

The renowned geologist Francois Matthes observed that this glacier is a "peculiar ice stream for its exceeding slenderness." From 11,000 to 11,500 feet the Kautz has its steepest gradient and forms an ice chute about 300 feet wide to the west of the Kautz Icecliff. Farther to the west of the chute another ring of icecliffs marks the edge of this chute. The main Kautz Icecliff, some of which overhangs the adjacent Wilson Headwall, is in a precarious position above the rock and snow slopes beneath it.

The Kautz route today is not the most popular way up Mount Rainier, yet it is the most used on the south flank. While the approach to a high camp is longer than routes passing by Camp Muir, the final climb is quite direct and relatively safe from falling ice débris once a party is in the chute. Furthermore, the route avoids the crowds of the Ingraham Glacier and Disappointment Cleaver routes. The Kautz route has a spectacular aspect in the 35-degree chute area, where there may be some bare ice, yet it should be considered generally an easy to moderate route for all but beginning climbers. The best climbing season is from May to early August. Early season climbers must be aware of potential avalance hazard.

In the 1940s the Kautz route was used by guided parties because of the closure of the Gibraltar Ledge (which collapsed in 1936). Climbs of the route prior to 1947 were generally reported as an easy ascent of the icecliff through a maze of terraces and pinnacles. The changing character of the icecliff area (between 11,300 and 12,000 feet) is such that it has formed a dangerous vertical barrier in some years, forcing climbers to ascend the more sensible ice chute to the west.

This route starts at Paradise. Ascend the Skyline Trail for 7/10 mile to about 6,000 feet (just below Glacier Vista). Follow a climber's path descending to the Nisqually Moraine Trail for about ½ mile to the eastern moraine of the Nisqually Glacier (about 5,500 feet). Cross the glacier near the 6,200-foot-level to a gully (may be snow or débris, depending on the season) on the opposite west flank. Ascend this gully (known as both the Wilson Gully and the Nisqually Fan) to the edge of the Wilson Glacier. Ascend centrally or along its western side to near 9,000 feet, then cross diagonally upward toward the base of the Wilson–Kautz rock cleaver (the Wapowety). Leave the Wilson Glacier near 9,500 feet and ascend The Turtle, a turtle-shaped snowfield that begins near 9,800 feet on Wapowety Cleaver. There are numerous campsites between 9,500 feet and 10,000 feet; some rock windbreaks have been erected. Time: Allow six hours to this site from Paradise.

Scurrying beneath the nose of the sporadically treacherous Kautz Icecliff, this party is returning from a successful climb and is just a hundred feet from Camp Hazard. (Joe Stermitz)

Unexpected Danger

The morning found us waking at 12:30 A.M. to clear skies and a full moon. The temperatures were unusually warm and there was a slight breeze. After the morning rituals we found our three rope teams stretching out to begin the long climb up "The Turtle" of the Kautz route.

The slopes were steep right out of camp so I started traversing, deciding where I'd make my switchback route. We were climbing for approximately twenty minutes, still about 2,000 feet below the Kautz icecliffs, at 9,300 feet.

Suddenly we heard ice or rockfall, a collapsing chunk of glacier, I assumed, which was probably going to spill onto either side of the ridge we were climbing, as it has previously.

Still 200 feet from the crest of the first roll and on my fifth switchback, I began to hear little buzzing noises, and squinted uphill to see what was up. Despite the full moon and starlit sky, we were unable to see anything—until it was upon us.

Ice chunks whizzed past our rope team.

Another camping option is Camp Hazard, just above 11,000 feet, about 200 feet below the Kautz Icecliff. While Camp Hazard has been considered safe by most climbers for many years, large pieces of ice have been witnessed falling extremely close to the camping sites. As warming trends continue to affect the Kautz Glacier, one could expect those sites to become more vulnerable to icefall. Time: Allow seven to nine hours to this site from Paradise.

While cooking dinner or resting in your tent or bivy sack, the volcanoes southward into Oregon will appear like solitary sentinels in fair weather. At this altitude, the panoramic vistas in all directions are enhanced by the curvature of the earth. At night the stars can exhibit a brilliance not seen at low altitudes, and the lights of towns and cities are marked by dots or clusters of color.

Make a headlamp start for the summit. It is best to leave your high camp with crampons and rope donned. Stopping to do this later in the chute, where it may seem logical to do so, exposes your party and those behind you to possible icefall and rockfall hazard.

From 11,200 feet descend westerly from the rock cleaver and skirt below the prominent lowest point of the icecliff (not a place to stop for a photo or breakfast break), then enter the upper Kautz ice chute. At all times keep a sharp lookout for falling débris. Continue to the chute's upper end, where it merges into the pinnacled area of the icecliff. Usually conditions are sun-cupped snow atop ice, but in late season there may be bare glacial ice in the chute (a party might wish to belay from ice screws then). As the chute widens, crevasses may force bearing left.

Now ascend the upper smooth portion of the Kautz Glacier, which is a dazzling white dome of néve to opposite Point Success. Then cross the saddle to the crater rim. From the saddle near where the Kautz Glacier levels out it is about 35 degrees true north to the crater rim.

Approach variation: From Van Trump Park ascend north to gentle slopes of Wapowety Cleaver. Follow these to Camp Hazard.

Approach variation: The Turtle Snowfield can also be accessed by climbing the Nisqually Glacier to about 7,200 feet and then negotiating the Wilson Glacier to the start of The Turtle.

Ascent variation: In some years it is possible to climb terraces in the 100- to 200-foot icecliff directly above high camp. A few ice screws may be desirable for protection. Keep a sharp lookout for falling débris in this area, in particular when below the icecliff.

Upper route variation: Climb the smooth slopes to the top of Wapowety Cleaver on the right (13,000 feet), then ascend the upper west (left) portion of the Nisqually Glacier to the crater. This variation is often less steep.

The Kautz route is considered a Grade II, but crowds on busy weekends and holidays, as well as objective hazards, can hinder progress. Bring a topographic map, compass, and wands. Take compass bearings on the ascent so that if clouds close in the descent will not become an epic. Because the upper Kautz is often heavily crevassed, it is important to understand how to do a crevasse extrication. Time: Six to eight hours from high camp.

Someone yelled, "Rock!" My pack took a hit from a sizeable block. A sound as if a blender had cut loose filled the air and huge chunks crashed through the rope teams.

I yelled instructions as best I could but, unable to do anything in the fury of the onslaught, I stood and watched as the horrible slow-motion events played out. When it was all over one climber had sustained a broken leg, another had a large bruise on his left leg, and another climber had a bruised wrist. All in all, we were lucky.

Art Rausch

The evening prior to climbing, Chuck Pell kicks steps to facilitate an easier climb the next morning. Icefall débris in the foreground reminds climbers to keep moving beneath the fringes of the overhanging Kautz Icecliff. *(Tom Stewart)*

12. Kautz Headwall, 1963

This headwall contains the glacier finger and the rock-and-snow face west of the upper part of the Kautz Glacier. It is bound on the west by the Kautz Cleaver and on the east by the upper portion of the Kautz Glacier. The first ascent was made by the expert trio of Patrik Callis, Dan Davis, and Don (Claunch) Gordon (all renowned for putting up hard new routes on Mount Robson) on July 8, 1963.

This is a much more challenging climb than the normal Kautz Glacier route and should only be attempted in good conditions. Exposure to rockfall is present in all but the last few feet of the route.

Between 12,500 feet and 13,200 feet on the Kautz Cleaver there are numerous options for climbing, allowing the mountaineer a choice of rock or snow. Here, Nick Farley approaches a short rock band at 12,500 feet. *(Alex Van Steen)*

From high camp at 9,800 feet on Wapowety Cleaver, use a short gully to descend onto the Kautz Glacier. Ascend the glacier to its head left of the icecliffs between the lower and upper Kautz. The greatest objective hazard of the route lies in traversing below these icecliffs. It is a wise idea to scout a route through the crevasses and débris from high camp so as to expedite travel beneath these icecliffs during the traditional nighttime start.

Ascend steep snow over and around rock bands. Slope steepness will depend mostly on snow conditions, but expect at least 50-degree slopes or steeper for short sections. The route is usually easiest to the west where the Success routes finish. Late-season ascents will involve some rock climbing through these bands. Follow snow slopes to Point Success, then bear northeast to the summit crater rim.

Route variation: Large late-season crevasses on the lower portion of the route may force the route far left and through a narrow snow gully penetrating the first prominent rock band.

Grade III or IV. Bring a few ice screws; some rock protection for late-season ascents is advisable. Helmets are an especially good idea as this headwall functions as a funnel for débris falling from above.

13. Kautz Cleaver, 1957

This rock ridge, which for some height separates the Kautz and Success Glaciers, merges with upper Success Cleaver near 12,000 feet. Claude E. Rusk and F. H. Kiser attained a high point on this route in 1905, but the first complete ascent was not done until September 1, 1957, by George Senner and Charles E. Robinson. Probably the lengthy approach has kept this route from popularity. The route is not particularly difficult.

Procedure

Drive the Nisqually Entrance park road for 4³⁄₁₀ miles beyond Longmire (at 3,650 feet). Hike the trail to Van Trump Park (3 miles).

From Van Trump Park ascend a short ridge (usually snow covered through midsummer) to 7,200 feet. Under early season snow, there is a great campsite here. Then maintain a slightly rising traverse west to the rocky ridges flanking the lower Kautz Glacier. Keep the traverse above the large bowl, which rapidly drops to the river valley below. Near 8,000 feet, descend onto the Kautz and cross on an upward diagonal to the base of Kautz Cleaver near 9,000 feet (it will be necessary to cross a crevassed area above a prominent icefall; conditions will vary here seasonally).

Chuck Pell at the entrance gully (near 9,000 feet) of the Kautz Cleaver *(Tom Stewart)*

Ascend on the left flank of the objective cleaver; some parties have followed the cleaver crest but found it slower and substantially more difficult. Attain a small saddle on the crest below a red gendarme (10,200 feet); here is a good bivouac site. Circle rightward around the gendarme, then left across the cleaver. One can ascend snow or névé along its left flank, but the broadening character of the cleaver permits progress between various minor ribs and gullies. There is route flexibility here. Continue to where the rock outcroppings broaden into upper Success Cleaver near 12,000 feet. Now ascend the merged Success–Kautz Cleaver route to Point Success.

There are several possible variations for climbing higher, but one should stay on the east side of the upper rock slabs. There are numerous short rock steps (depending on route selection) that protect easily with modern rock gear. The compass bearing from Point Success to the crater rim is 50 degrees true north. Grade II.

Bring some rock gear. Time: Eight to ten hours from high camp to the crater rim.

Approach variation: Approach as for Success Cleaver, then bear eastward toward the Kautz Cleaver.

RMI Expedition Seminar camped on the "ice balcony" at 9,800 feet at the base of the Success Glacier Headwall *(Alex Van Steen)*

14. Success Glacier Couloir, Eastern Couloir of the Success Headwall, 1960

This route, also known as "Success Finger," climbs a snow finger above the head of the Success Glacier. This glacier (a Kautz tributary) heads in a cirque against the rock flanks of Point Success. The first ascent was made by George Senner and Dick Wahlstrom on July 17, 1960.

Opposite: Morning view into the Nisqually drainage from high on the route (about 11,000 feet) *(Alex Van Steen)*

Procedure

See the Success Cleaver route for approach information. From lower Success Cleaver near 7,500 feet, bear east and cross the small Pyramid Glacier to 8,500 feet. There is a good campsite just east of the cleaver between the Pyramid and Success Glaciers. Then ascend the Success Glacier to its head. At 10,200 feet a bergschrund may have to be crossed (a seasonal problem). At this location a broad snow finger (the eastern of the three main snow fingers above the glacier) tapers to rock outcroppings at the 12,000-foot-level. With ample snow, a narrow and exposed bivouac site exists here. Then continue per Kautz Cleaver.

Grade II. Pickets or ice screws may assist crossing the bergschrund. Bring some rock gear for the upper Success–Kautz rock bands. Time: Eight to ten hours from high camp to the summit.

15. Middle Finger of Success, Central Couloir of the Success Headwall, 1987

This route climbs the central snow finger of the Success Glacier Headwall. The probable first ascent was made in 1987 by James Couch and party.

Climber traversing beneath the lower Kautz Icefall at 7,500 feet en route to the Success Glacier *(Alex Van Steen)*

Procedure

From a high camp at the Success–Pyramid divide (8,500 feet), approach and cross the bergschrund at 10,400 feet. Ascend to near the couloir head at 11,500 feet. Then cross over, keeping to the right. Follow the right side of the rib through rock bands to 13,000 feet on upper Success Cleaver and finally to Point Success.

Grade II. Brings some pickets and some rock gear and a helmet. Time: Eight to ten hours from high camp to the summit.

16. Fickle Finger of Success, Western Couloir of the Success Headwall, 1997

This westernmost route is the shortest of the three couloir routes climbing the Success Glacier Headwall, and joins upper Success Cleaver at 11,600 feet. On the first ascent, Alex Van Steen and Richard Alpert led a Rainier Mountaineering party of four (David Branton, Mark Kelly, Steve Northern, and Pete Laird) to a summit camp on July 25, 1997.

Procedure

An approach can be made from Van Trump Park (the traverse beneath the lower Kautz Glacier icefall at 7,500 feet to the Success–Pyramid divide at 8,500 feet) or via Indian Henrys Hunting Grounds to lower Success Cleaver. Then ascend the Success Glacier to a possible high camp, an inobvious "balcony" at 9,800 feet (the base of the Success Glacier Headwall). This camp is somewhat protected from possible rockfall by the bergschrund that separates the glacier from the snow couloirs above. From the bergschrund (at 10,000 feet) to the confluence with the standard Success Cleaver route (at 11,600 feet, where Success Cleaver traverses east toward Kautz Cleaver), the couloir is consistently moderate of angle (40 degrees). Owing to the heavy snow year, the 1997 party found the rock bands on the upper mountain, which are normally exposed at this time of the year, to be simply steep snow climbing (no steeper than 50 degrees). Camp was made on the summit and descent was via the standard Disappointment Cleaver route.

Late-season ascents of all the Success Glacier Headwall routes increase both the difficulty of the bergschrund crossing at 10,200 feet and the incidence of rockfall, which may be unrelenting. Grade II. Brings some pickets, rock gear, and a helmet. Time: Eight to ten hours from high camp to the summit.

A beautiful January morning above Indian Henrys Hunting Ground highlights Success Cleaver. *(Tom Stewart)*

17. Success Cleaver, 1905

This is the great rock spur on the mountain's southwest flank. It leads to 14,158-foot Point Success (first attained on the 1870 Stevens–Van Trump ascent). The cleaver begins at the 6,500-foot saddle north of Pyramid Peak and in late summer can become nearly an all-rock route. While most of the cleaver is protected from rockfall by its projection, there may be a few unpleasant traverses after surface snow melts.

Amazingly, large slabs of snow and rock have been witnessed falling away from the upper ridges from the 9,000-foot elevation on up. The route is not usually difficult, but the approach is moderately long. Most climbing parties carrying sleeping or bivouac gear make a traverse of Mount Rainier to descend by another route. Many parties choose not to rope up on the cleaver, but do rope up on the crossing from Point Success to the crater rim, where crevasses exist. Steep, firm snow (perfect climbing conditions), however, generally warrants the use of rope for all but the most experienced parties.

In the summer of 1905 Ernest Dudley and John Glascock, members of a Sierra Club outing, made the entire ascent from Paradise in one day (they traversed intervening glaciers and reached the summit of Point Success on the evening of July 24, then continued to the crater for a cold night). The two climbers then descended to Camp Muir after being without food or sleep for thirty-five hours. (This tactic is not recommended, especially if the party is not acclimated to higher altitudes.)

Procedure

Hike the Kautz Creek Trail from the road to Paradise at 3 miles (2,400 feet) beyond the Nisqually Park Entrance to Indian Henrys Hunting Ground (5½ miles).

From near Mirror Lake (about 5,600 feet) ascend meadows northeast via a climber's trail and traverse snowfields around the northern base of Pyramid Peak to reach the broad rock crest of the objective cleaver. Note that there are good high camp locations near 8,300 feet and just above 9,500 feet.

Just below the 9,500-foot-level the cleaver forms the first of two major steps; keep right when passing both of these. At the top of the second step there is a sandy area that has been used for a bivouac.

Above 10,000 feet one must pass several crumbly pinnacles before the cleaver steepens to force the route to the east. Near 11,000 feet, angle below cliffs across a succession of chutes (near their tops) into a large snow couloir that broadens at the top. Bear right for the shoulder skyline at 12,000 feet, at the confluence with Kautz Cleaver. Above 12,000 feet one can vary the way considerably, but higher, expect at least one short rock pitch. Continue upward on a traverse over rock or snow, keeping on the east flank to Point Success. Most parties will want to continue to the crater rim and the true summit. Cross the intervening saddle. Grade II. Time: Seven hours from high camp to Point Success.

A climber enters the steeper gullies used to traverse off the cleaver and onto the upper Success Glacier Headwall. *(Don Goodman)*

Approach variation: Begin at the road to Paradise, at Christine Falls (3,600 feet). Hike via Comet Falls to 6,000 feet in Van Trump Park, then bear leftward toward the base of the Kautz Glacier. Near 8,000 feet, traverse west, cross the Pyramid Glacier, and reach Success Cleaver near 8,400 feet.

As the sun sets, a climber approaches the 9,500-foot bivouac platform.
(Terry LaFrance)

18. South Tahoma Headwall, Central Route, 1963

The South Tahoma Glacier, located on the southwest flank of Mount Rainier between the Success and Tahoma Cleavers, is featured in its upper portion by a quite steep and recessed headwall. Here is a cirque-born glacier, nourished by both avalanches and direct snowfall.

The headwall of this cirque extends from bergschrunds near 10,300 feet and steepens to Point Success. Because of rockfall potential from exposed bands, a climb of the headwall should only be done during optimal conditions; these usually seem to occur only in late spring or early summer. The headwall was first climbed by Steve Marts and Fred Beckey on July 12, 1963. There have been other ascents, and some variations in the upper portion,

A view from Success Cleaver toward the crux difficulties of the South Tahoma Headwall (Jason Edwards)

U.S. Military In a Blizzard

During the week of March 19–23, 1989, a ten-person army unit climbed from Paradise to the Camp Muir area to test equipment and men in a winter mountaineering environment. Shortly after encountering blizzard conditions, three members of the group were sent back because of frostbite, fatigue, and hypothermia; they became disoriented and descended the Paradise Glacier instead of the Muir Snowfield. Despite the danger of travel on glaciated terrain, the group chose not to rope together. Although they stopped for an extended period to melt snow for water and soup, they did not set up a tent or dig a snow cave for the night. Choosing instead to continue walking slowly, they were able to return to Paradise on the morning of the third day, just as rescuers were preparing to initiate a ground search.

Military training programs are not without problems, and in this case the weather conditions at the Muir Snowfield were underestimated. Accidents in North American Mountaineering (edited by Jed Williamson and published annually by

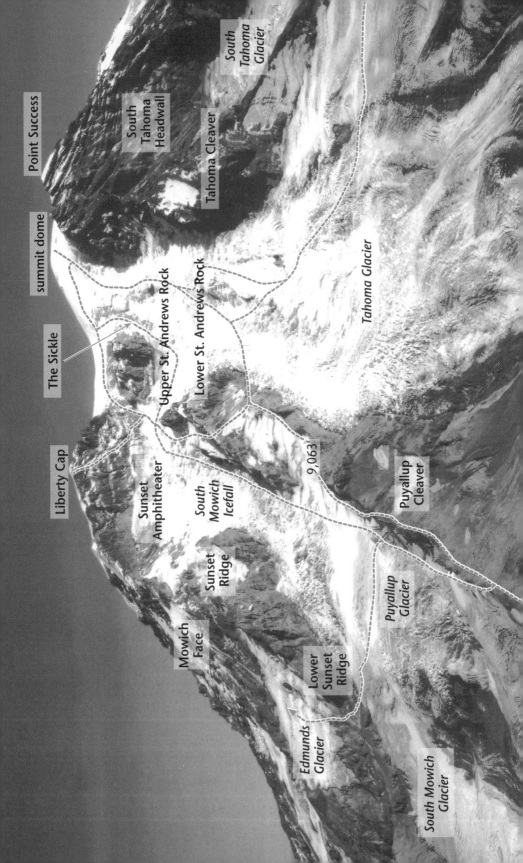

Point Success

summit dome

South Tahoma Headwall

Tahoma Cleaver

South Tahoma Glacier

The Sickle

Upper St. Andrews Rock

Lower St. Andrews Rock

Tahoma Glacier

Liberty Cap

Sunset Amphitheater

South Mowich Icefall

9,063

Puyallup Cleaver

Mowich Face

Sunset Ridge

Puyallup Glacier

Lower Sunset Ridge

Edmunds Glacier

South Mowich Glacier

but the climb is not commonly done. As of 1999, it may have seen as few as a dozen ascents.

A Marine Corps aircraft crashed on the lower South Tahoma Glacier in December 1946, and for some time this section of the glacier was closed as a memorial.

Procedure

Approach this route as for Success Cleaver or Tahoma Cleaver.

From a camp on Success Cleaver near 8,300 feet, traverse north to the objective glacier; it may be necessary to make a short descent at some point. Choose a line near the center or near the north side of the glacier, and work through crevasses as necessary. After crossing the bergschrund, ascend directly up the face; keep right of the curving couloir that slants down from the upper left portion of the face. Climb a left-slanting ice ramp (below a small icecliff) to a corner near the top of Point Success (14,158 feet). Now easy snow and néve slopes lead to the top.

Grade IV; bring some ice screws and pickets. Time: Seven hours on the face.

the American Alpine Club) concluded that the personnel on the training mission "had flunked navigation, passed survival, and flunked communication." Descending from high above timberline in blizzard and whiteout conditions can be a harrowing experience, and one that has resulted in past tragedies on both Mount Rainier and Mount Hood. Fortunately, these men were very fit and did make it to the road.

Tahoma Glacier climbers bivouac on Puyallup Cleaver; Puyallup Glacier in view. *(Joe Catellani)*

19. South Tahoma Headwall, Western Route, 1982

Another route on this headwall was climbed in 1982 and again in 1989.

On the left portion of the headwall, Sean Meehan and Todd Woolridge made a climb on May 24, 1982, by going diagonally left up broad steep snow below the rock bands near the crest of Tahoma Cleaver; then they climbed several ice slopes and rock bands to Point Success.

Another similar headwall climb, possibly with only minor variations, was done by Buce Anderson and Steve Risse on June 26, 1989, following the same obvious gully and ramp system on the left side of the face. At about 12,600 feet, they followed a narrower gully back right, directly toward the top of the headwall. Two short rock bands in this section required pitons for safety. Complete the climb at a corner just below Point Success.

20. Tahoma Cleaver, 1959

Separating the Tahoma and South Tahoma Glaciers is a quite prominent spur, the Tahoma Cleaver. The climb of this cleaver seems to be seldom done, probably because of the changing technical problems, and the fact that this is a long climb on the mountain. In the recent past this route, or a variation of it, has been climbed solo in winter by a quiet Spokane climber.

The route can be demanding and should only be attempted under cool temperatures and with good snow conditions. The route on this cleaver begins at 9,000 feet and extends to the northwest corner of Point Success.

Because a section of rock near 12,000 feet has broken away, climbers may be forced to the variation described. The first ascent of the route was made by Klindt Vielbig, Tony Hovey, Don Keller, Paul Bellamy, and Herb Steiner on June 7, 1959.

Procedure

Drive the West Side Road to its closure (3 miles), then hike the road to the Marine Memorial near Round Pass (3½ miles). A short trail heads east to reach the South Puyallup River, and on to South Puyallup Camp (2½ miles). Follow the Wonderland Trail (joining here) about 1⅗ miles around Emerald Ridge, then cross below the terminus of the Tahoma Glacier on moraine and outwash débris. Now hike east into the principal broad gully splitting Glacier Island, which is a long slope in early season. Continue to the broad northern edge of the South Tahoma Glacier. Follow the glacier, keeping to the right of several rock islands and buttresses to about 9,200 feet. Then proceed upslope to a small snow col at 10,000 feet, just above the base of a reddish rock tower. Note that the last good campsite on this cleaver is found at 11,600 feet. Time: Allow eight to ten hours from the road.

Gene Prater leads through a rimed ice shelf at 12,800 feet on the Tahoma Cleaver. *(Tom Stewart)*

Proceed upward on moderate snow slopes toward a prominent rock spire (11,700 feet) on the ridge; pass some 200 feet below it on the right and traverse diagonally across long, steep south-facing snow slopes toward the huge black buttress that blocks the crest. Gain the narrow snow ridge about 100 yards before the buttress, then follow to its base near 12,000 feet. Around the north side of the buttress there is a short, solid rock pitch; this leads to a steep, rounded 500-foot slope bearing to the buttress crest left of the massive squarish tower. From a snow saddle bear northeast on a steeply inclined snow ramp to its end at 13,700 feet (where it drops off to the Tahoma Glacier). Follow steep ledges around the corner (right) for 300 feet. Cross broken ice to the summit icecap. Now climb northeast to the crater rim. Grade IV; bring ice screws and rock pitons. Time: Eleven hours from high camp.

Ascent variation via 1968 route, Stewart's lower traverse: By Dan Davis, Gene Prater, Tom Stewart, and Steve Marts on June 16, 1968.

The second ascent party of 1968 found the huge black buttress at 12,000 feet to be heavily eroded, forming a vertical wall. Seeing this, they then made a traversing ascent up steep snow and ice slopes below the high vertical rock band for a considerable distance. Where the ice joins cliffs, they scaled two rock pitches (exposed class 4), which are long, steep, and loose, to surmount the band and meet the original route.

Approach variation: Hike the South Puyallup River Trail from the West Side Road (at 7½ miles) to the Wonderland Trail (1½ miles). Then continue to Emerald Ridge. Continue to the Tahoma Glacier moraine and proceed northeast to the lower south fringe of the glacier. At about 7,000 feet bear toward the north edge of the South Tahoma Glacier.

Gene Prater, Dan Davis, and Steve Marts start the technical climbing on the Tahoma Cleaver in May 1968. Don't look for the two rock towers above their heads as landmarks; they no longer exist. *(Tom Stewart)*

21. Tahoma Glacier, 1891

This massive glacier tumbles from the depression west of the summit cone through a narrow gap and descends some 4½ miles to below timberline. In the nineteenth century the Tahoma and South Tahoma Glaciers flowed in wide detours around Glacier Island and united below it.

In early summer the Tahoma Glacier provides one of Mount Rainier's most direct routes from timberline, but by August it can be quite badly broken. This is an excellent glacier route—one that should see more traffic. But allow one and a half days for any of the optional approaches. Longer approaches are good acclimatization!

The first ascent of the glacier was made by Philemon Van Trump, Alfred Drewry, Dr. Warren Riley, and Riley's deerhound on August 11, 1891.

Opposite: Thrilling traverses lead climbers toward the more technical sections of the route high above the Tahoma Glacier. *(Tom Stewart)*

Procedure

Because the West Side Road is currently closed to vehicles at 3 miles, the approach is longer than in previous years, but there are still two reasonable approaches. For the first approach, take the Kautz Creek Trail to Indian Henrys Hunting Ground, then continue up Success Cleaver to a saddle at about 8,400 feet, just beyond Pyramid Peak. Drop off the cleaver and then traverse the South Tahoma and Tahoma Glaciers near 8,500 to 8,600 feet to reach Puyallup Cleaver and a campsite. This traverse climbs slightly, crossing Tahoma Cleaver. It is roughly 3 miles (directly) from Indian Henrys Hunting Ground to the Puyallup Cleaver.

For the second approach, hike the West Side Road to the Marine Memorial near Round Pass (3½ miles). A short trail heads east to reach the South Puyallup River and on to South Puyallup Camp (2½ miles).

This approach gives you three options. For the first option, head north on the Wonderland Trail (crossing the suspension bridge) about 1 mile, then traverse east to the northern flank of the Tahoma Glacier and Puyallup Cleaver. Eventually drop onto the glacier (above 9,000 feet); this may be difficult in late season.

The second option follows the Puyallup Cleaver farther than the first. From just below Tokaloo Rock, keep south of this feature on the cleaver and continue up the crest to an 8,000-foot notch. Take the Puyallup Glacier around the north flank of the large rock buttress (9,063 feet) on the cleaver, then return to the cleaver (9,200 feet). Here is a good campsite. Time: Allow one day or more from the road.

Ascend the Puyallup Glacier just left of the cleaver to a large snowfield (near 10,000 feet) that drops south through a break. Make a diagonal descent south onto the Tahoma Glacier, then choose the best line of ascent. It might do well to study the crevasse patterns on the previous day to identify beforehand the best line to take when climbing in the darkness or in poor light. Climbers have found it best to ascend the steep section near the center or just right of center. From the top of the glacier, where it slopes onto the summit icefield, the bearing is close to 90 degrees true north to reach the crater rim. If a descent is planned via the Tahoma, a few wands at key spots could be useful.

The third and final option for the West Side Road approach is to access the Tahoma Glacier via Emerald Ridge and Glacier Island (see the approach for Tahoma Cleaver).

Some parties have descended the Tahoma Glacier "Sickle" to avoid crevasses on the main glacier (see the "Sickle" variation). The entire ascent is a Grade II. Time: Six to nine hours from high camp to the crater rim.

St. Andrews Rock variation: In late summer the main glacier may be badly crevassed below 11,000 feet. An option is to scramble over lower St. Andrews Rock (easy but loose) and then continue along the edge of the South Mowich Glacier (around the north side of upper St. Andrews Rock; if crevasses bar the way, climb over the rock).

South Mowich Icefall and Tahoma Glacier "Sickle" variation: This variation was first climbed by Leroy Ritchie, Larry Heggerness, Allan Van Buskirk, Edward Drues, Bob Walton, and Monte and Mark Haun on June 8, 1958. From Puyallup Cleaver near

8,000 feet work across the Puyallup Glacier to above Colonnade Ridge. Climb the South Mowich Glacier Icefall to the upper end of upper St. Andrews Rock (11,200 feet); this usually is a good route only in early season because of glacier chaos. Now bear south and ascend the sickle-shaped trough at the extreme north end of the upper Tahoma Glacier. The "Sickle" can be a good early-season variation. Time: Eleven hours from an 8,000-foot camp. It should be noted that if crevasses are open or bridges are not in good condition on the descent, one can down-climb upper St. Andrews Rock (crumbly but reasonable).

22. Sunset Amphitheater–Tahoma Glacier Icecap, 1937

At the head of the South Mowich Glacier is a unique west-facing cirque, a vast reservoir of ice nearly 1 mile wide and some 2,000 feet higher than any similar cirque on the mountain. The cirque headwall of Sunset Amphitheater begins at 12,500 feet, then maintains a constant steepness to Liberty Cap, the upper slopes of Sunset Ridge, and the icecap at the western edge of the upper Tahoma Glacier. The amphitheater wall is characterized by furrows carved by both rock and ice avalanches from the upper headwall.

Although the amphitheater is similar to those resulting merely from glacier erosion, studies indicate the overall feature is a scar probably formed by repeated landslides. Glacier erosion, however, must have abetted the hollowing of this broad cirque. The ice reservoir beneath the headwall descends as the narrow South Mowich Icefall. This ice cascade then divides to send a portion of its volume to the Puyallup Glacier. In spite of this loss, the South Mowich Glacier attains a length of nearly 4 miles, while the Puyallup remains on a higher bedrock level and expands to about 1 mile in width.

This rugged and seldom visited flank of Mount Rainier was virtually unknown until the late 1930s, when two park rangers, J. Wendell Trosper and Fred Thieme, made the first ascent of the Sunset Amphitheater on July 13, 1937. This ascent was a spirited effort over new ground, one that involved both route-finding problems and technical climbing.

Procedure

Take the same long approach as for the Tahoma Glacier route to the Puyallup Cleaver campsite at 9,200 feet. Here climb the upper Puyallup Glacier to its head, then climb over lower St. Andrews

A First Experience on Mount Rainier

(Note: The writer has been kept anonymous. Names have been changed to protect the innocent. Source: A Boealps newsletter.)

July 29. We've spent the last week sorting out gear and I'm really excited. I've been training all season. I'm in shape from running hills and from our Mount Adams climb two weeks ago.

I leave work early to meet my husband Archibald and his friend Ulysses at a Seattle parking lot. At the White River ranger station we are told that the campground is already full, but we locate a spot not so far up the trail.

We pitch the tent on what appears to be the middle of an elk trail. Pointing this out to the guys, they assure me that no elk will be using this trail tonight because there will be a tent on it. Trying to sleep, I wonder if an elk's hoof is bigger than a person's head. And would an elk see the tent in the dark?

The next day we pitch our tent above Steamboat Prow. The camp is pretty full, and we have a

Climbers work their way up the slopes of Sunset Ridge. *(Don Goodman)*

Rock; should crevasses prove a problem, climb over the rock's crest. Ascend the slopes of Sunset Amphitheater to the bergschrund across the steep slope; the 1937 party crossed the bergschrund on a tilted ice plug, then cut steps, using ice piton protection. Anticipate problems; changing conditions may require that a different procedure is taken here.

Now climb and traverse steep ice to the north end of the upper Tahoma Glacier icecap (at 12,500 feet). The Trosper–Thieme party climbed to the icecap by stemming a huge longitudinal crevasse to reach the upper glacier's surface south of Liberty Cap. Because of changing conditions, getting onto the icecap now (sixty years later) could be quite different (ranging from easy to impossible). Unless the summit objective is Liberty Cap, cross the summit icecap eastward to the crater rim.

Grade III or IV; include some ice screws in your equipment. Time: Twelve hours from St. Andrews Rock to Liberty Cap (should be less if the icecap is not a big problem).

23. Sunset Amphitheater Headwall, 1965

This headwall is the gullied cirque directly beneath Liberty Cap, one that had been avoided by climbers until most of Mount Rainier's other technical routes were completed. As a route, the headwall can be quite dangerous, but in good conditions it is relatively safe for a fast party; note that some rockfall was encountered on the first ascent. The route would be a poor choice if there is apparent avalanche danger. The first ascent was made by Jim Wickwire, Gene Prater, Dave Mahre, Fred Stanley, and Don McPherson on July 24, 1965.

Approach the headwall as for Sunset Amphitheater–Tahoma Glacier Icecap. Cross the headwall bergschrund while still beneath the great icecliff, then make a leftward traverse along the top of the bergschrund on rock and ice. In 1965 a hard section on rock led around a corner to the deep couloir separating the icecliff from the headwall (this is an avalanche hazard area).

Cross the couloir to the open face, then climb diagonally across the large snow patches. Now cross leftward to a third pitch and up a long snow ramp for several hundred feet to the steep rock buttress that lines the headwall crest; this ramp was reported as safe. At the upper end of the ramp, cross right to a narrow, twisting, 500-foot gully between two rock walls. This tactic allows an exit from the headwall to a completion some 200 feet below the top of Liberty Cap. It also should be noted that an ascent variation via a plumb line recently has been claimed (but not documented). Grade III or IV; bring ice screws and rock pitons. Time: Seven hours from camp at 9,200 feet.

24. Sunset Ridge, 1938

Sunset Ridge is a long, undulating spur extending from opposite the confluence of the Puyallup and South Mowich Glaciers (8,500 feet) to the crest of Liberty Cap. The ridge is a prominent snow

fantastic view of the privy. It's not much of a privy—just a couple of plywood boards blocking the wind on one side of a hole in the snow. I'm glad I had thought to sew a zipper all the way down the crotch of my pants. I'm even more glad that I packed my Tupperware.

We turn in before the sun goes down. There are lots of people in the camp and it's noisy. Besides, I can't help thinking of the icefall we just witnessed. We wake up at midnight and all I can do is ask how far we are from coffee. We rope up … it's colder up on this exposed mountainside than it was near the tent and hot coffee. I get chilled and feel a little sick before too long. Adding a sweater takes the chill off, but the granola bar won't go down and I spit it out. I feel awful, because I know I will be up here practically forever. Later, seeing what somebody else had left behind, I don't feel quite so bad.

As we round a crevasse, I can't help noticing its hugeness. My headlamp illuminates the whole of the inside—I am afraid and awed. We find a good spot for a short rest. About an hour later we seem pretty near the top, and I think it won't be long now. Step, rest. Step, rest. At some

Sunset
Ridge

Edmunds
Headwall

Mowich Face

Ptarmigan Ridge

Liberty Cap

Liberty
Cap
Glacier

1935

North
Mowich
Glacier

10,310'

Curtis Ridge

Willis Wall

Liberty Ridge

crest, easily noted from afar, separating the Sunset Amphitheater from the expanse of Mowich Face. The ridge broadens below 12,000 feet and is actually composed of two lower ridges separated by a steep snowfield and gully; even lower is a lobe of the South Mowich Glacier that rests on the ridge.

As a climbing route, Sunset Ridge is an attractive proposition, and it seems to be gaining popularity. While the climb is long and has several steep sections, much of the route's gradient is moderate. Up to about 12,000 feet the climb takes the moderately steep snow gully slopes north of the main ridge crest (near the center of the broader lower half of the ridge). A direct ascent variation would be much longer.

It is surprising that Sunset Ridge was not attempted prior to 1938—when more difficult routes such as Liberty Ridge and Ptarmigan Ridge had already been climbed. The first ascent was made by Lyman Boyer, Arnold Campbell, and Don Woods on August 27 and 28, 1938. The party chose to chop a bivouac platform at 11,000 feet, then continue the following day. The highly coveted winter ascent of Sunset Ridge was finally accomplished after numerous attempts by Jim Yoder and Kevin Buselmeier in February 1997. The pair, equipped with a strong support team, accessed the route via the Paul Peak Trail and the South Mowich River drainage and climbed the route to its junction with Ptarmigan Ridge before weather turned them around.

point the sun rises, and the world turns pink for a moment. I think I'm in heaven.

I'd been warned these climbs are sometimes best appreciated after the fact. Right now my overriding sensation is fatigue. My grand idea of walking over to plant my footprints on the crater seems frivolous.

Finally we reach the trail back toward the parking lot. As we plod along, we pass a family hiking up the trail. A tired teenage boy asks how far the trail goes. I turn around, pointing to the mountain behind me and say, "All the way to the top."

Procedure

See the approach directions for the Tahoma Glacier to access the 8,000-foot notch on Puyallup Cleaver. Traverse the Puyallup Glacier at the same level to reach the upper end of Colonnade Ridge (between the Puyallup and South Mowich Glaciers) where a high camp can be made at 8,300 feet. Time: Allow all day from the road, perhaps with an intermediate camp. Note that an alternate camp location has been used at the 9,200-foot divide between the South Mowich and Edmunds Glaciers.

Descend to and cross the South Mowich Glacier. Aim for the lowest cliff-corner of Sunset Ridge and turn it. Then climb the moderately steep side-lobe of the glacier to its upper bergschrund. Cross the bergschrund and ascend the long, moderately steep snow and ice gully to gain the ridge crest overlooking Sunset Amphitheater at 12,000 feet. From this position, traverse the ridge crest to a minor saddle. This section may be crumbling rock and loose; in early summer it may be solidly snow covered. Now ascend the unbroken upper 1,000 feet of the ridge to a final broad néve

slope leading directly to Liberty Cap (14,112 feet). Grade III. Time: Nine to twelve hours from high camp. Note that there are two known major variations, probably of comparable difficulty.

Ascent variation, Sunset Amphitheater–Sunset Ridge, 1939: First done by J. Wendell Trosper and Hans Grage in early August, 1939, this variation traverses north from above St. Andrews Rock, then ascends a steep snow slope, which joins the South Mowich Glacier with Sunset Ridge at 12,000 feet. The reported time to Liberty Cap was seven hours from high camp.

Ascent variation, South Flank of Edmunds Glacier Headwall, 1963: First done by Gene Prater, Dave Mahre, Jim Wickwire, Fred Dunham, and Fred Stanley on May 31, 1963, this variation stays left of the lower portion of the Sunset Ridge route and takes the south flank of the Edmunds Glacier Headwall. Access is gained by a saddle on the lower left edge of Sunset Ridge, above the bergschrund at the head of the lower headwall; climb upward to bear back to the original route just below where it meets the main ridge crest.

A climber enjoys the steepening slopes of the Edmunds Headwall of the Mowich Face. *(Jim Nelson)*

Mowich Face

The challenge of the roughly triangular-shaped incline known as the Mowich Face lies in the framework of its two prominent spurs—Ptarmigan and Sunset Ridges. The face rises 4,000 feet to its apex at the 13,500-foot snow dome west of Liberty Cap. Its hanging ice feeds the Edmunds and North Mowich Glaciers; The Edmunds heads on the southern portion of the Mowich Face, while the North Mowich is fed by two lobes above the 8,000-foot-level (one heads at 10,500 feet against Ptarmigan Ridge and one heads centrally under the face).

In its lower portion the Mowich Face is almost 1 mile in width. Characterized by steep ice slopes, there are several conspicuous icecliffs. One immense icecliff hangs midway up the central right portion of the face, while another caps the north half. In this section there is a long and precipitous icefall.

Since the first climb of the face, in 1957, other distinct route lines have been made, all of similar length and difficulty; in addition, the routes have minor variations. The apparent steepness of the face as seen head-on from the forested Puget Sound lowlands undoubtedly discouraged earlier attempts. While any route on the face is an exceptional climb, in reality most of the incline is not over 40 degrees, and only short stretches exceed 50 degrees. The face should only be climbed under cold and firm conditions. New snowfall could create dangerous avalanche conditions; late-season exposure of rock bands could set off undesirable rockfalls. While the face has been descended, most parties return by the Tahoma Glacier or make a carry over via the crater rim.

Routes on the Mowich Face are listed from right to left, beginning with the 1957 climb (termed the Edmunds Headwall). The other routes have taken the names Central Mowich Face, North Mowich Headwall, and North Mowich Face Icefall.

25. Edmunds Headwall, 1957

This pioneering route, on the right (south) portion of the face, was climbed by John Rupley, Donald (Claunch) Gordon, Fred Beckey, Tom Hornbein, and Herb Staley on June 23, 1957. The shortest access is via the directions given for the Tahoma Glacier and Sunset Ridge routes. A longer option is to hike the West Side Road and the 2½-mile trail to Klapatche Park. Continue to St. Andrews Park (⁷⁄₁₀ mile south), then ascend snowfields and ridges to the crest of the Puyallup Cleaver just below Tokaloo Rock. Keep south here and then continue to an 8,000-foot notch on Puyallup Cleaver. Then traverse the Puyallup Glacier at the same level to reach the upper end of Colonnade Ridge, where a high camp can be made at 8,300 feet (allow one day or more from the road). Descend slightly, then cross the South Mowich Glacier and bypass the lowest cliff corner of Sunset Ridge.

Ascend the lower ice lobe of the Sunset Ridge route to the rock divide at 9,200

Opposite: Mount Rainier from the northwest (Mowich Face)
(USGS, courtesy Geophysical Institute, University of Alaska Fairbanks)

Point Success

Columbia Crest

Liberty Cap

Sunset Ridge

Upper St. Andrews Rock

Lower St. Andrews Rock

Colonnade Ridge

South Mowich Glacier

Mowich Face

Edmunds Glacier

Ptarmigan Ridge

North Mowich Glacier

10,310'

9,600'

9,200'

9,200'

1

2

3

4

1. Edmunds Headwall
2. Central Mowich Face
3. North Mowich Headwall
4. North Mowich Face Icefall

feet, overlooking the Edmunds Glacier. Make a short descent and then traverse below an icefall during a ½-mile crossing of the upper Edmunds Glacier. Beyond a little icefall turn upward: A flat-topped rock island on the left (9,600 feet), separating the Edmunds from the North Mowich Glacier, provides an alternate campsite. Time: Allow at least a very full day to get to this location.

Ascend to and cross the main bergschrund. There is little description needed from here. Kick in your crampons and plug away with one or two tools. Liberty Cap will gradually appear closer. The condition of the snow and ice may vary considerably on the way to the upper portion of Sunset Ridge. Once here, Liberty Cap is not far. Grade III or IV; bring some ice screws and perhaps pickets. Time: Allow nine to twelve hours from Colonnade Ridge to Liberty Cap.

26. Central Mowich Face, 1966

This route ascends the North Mowich Glacier to the north of the 1957 route. A high camp can be made at 9,600 feet on the flat-topped rock island separating the Edmunds and North Mowich Glaciers—one used by the first ascent party of Dee

Sunburst backlights a climber on the Edmunds Headwall. *(Jim Nelson)*

Molenaar, Gene Prater, Jim Wickwire, and Dick Pargeter on July 24, 1966.

Chuck Patzer and Chuck Crenshaw climb near 13,000 feet on the steep exit of the Central Mowich Face. *(Tom Stewart)*

Reach the face as for the Edmunds Headwall, then from the rock island make a climbing traverse toward the objective line. Cross the bergschrund where practical, then ascend 45-degree slopes to an alcove below the rock bands at 12,500 feet. Climb the lowest of three bands by a 15-foot cliff at the waist of an ice hourglass; the 1966 party found a 40-foot rock pitch here. Then traverse north along a steep, narrow snow-covered ledge and around an exposed corner, where the ledge broadens to steep ice. This ice narrows to a chute that separates the rock bands from the icecap bulge on the north (front-pointing and ice screws may be necessary, depending on conditions). The chute provides a direct exit to the rounded crest of upper Ptarmigan Ridge. Grade III or IV; bring ice screws and perhaps pickets.

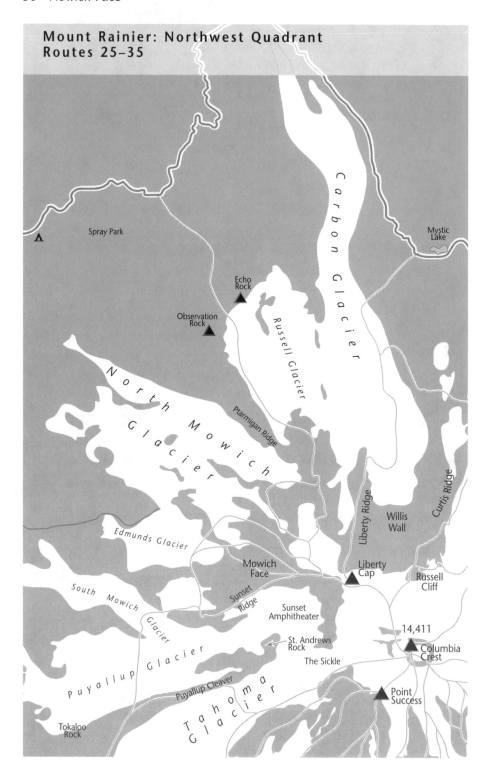

Mount Rainier: Northwest Quadrant
Routes 25–35

Spray Park

Mystic Lake

Echo Rock

Carbon Glacier

Observation Rock

Russell Glacier

North Mowich Glacier

Ptarmigan Ridge

Edmunds Glacier

Liberty Ridge

Willis Wall

Curtis Ridge

South Mowich Glacier

Mowich Face

Sunset Ridge

Liberty Cap

Russell Cliff

Sunset Amphitheater

St. Andrews Rock

14,411

Puyallup Glacier

The Sickle

Columbia Crest

Point Success

Puyallup Cleaver

Tokaloo Rock

Tahoma Glacier

Time: Seven hours from the rock island bivouac site to Liberty Cap.

Ascent variation, 1967 finish (exit right): This variation was done by Del Young, Bill Sumner, Bill Cockerham, and Ed Marquart on July 4, 1967.

From below the base of the rock bands make a diagonal right traverse (below the rock band system), then climb directly up steep ice slopes at the apex of the face; extensive use of ice screws may be needed. This variation is more difficult and direct than the original climb.

27. North Mowich Headwall, 1968

This headwall on the north third of the Mowich Face is probably the most serious of the three routes. There are technical problems—falling rock and ice hazard. There is a significant rock cliff near the bottom of the headwall and several more at the top, beneath the capping ice.

The first ascent was made by Mike Heath, Dan Davis, Mead Hargis, and Bill Cockerham on July 22, 1968. Make the approach as for the Edmunds Headwall route. A short climbing traverse past the little icefall on the upper Edmunds leads to a rock outcrop at 9,200 feet between the Edmunds and North Mowich Glaciers; this is a good bivouac site.

Traverse the North Mowich about ½ mile, bearing toward a concave bowl at the route's beginning (this bowl is directly beneath the upper icecliff). Cross the bergschrund and then ascend a difficult hourglass that cuts the lower rock band. Continue on snow and ice to the rock cliff just below the right end of the icecliff. Climb rightward to beneath the right end of the icecliff where the ice steepens. The 1968 party then climbed a 50-foot vertical rock band (hard class 5—could be aided). Then reach the ice just right of the icecliff. The final 600 feet of climbing is steep ice slopes; then round off onto upper Ptarmigan Ridge and continue to Liberty Cap. Grade IV; bring ice screws and some rock pitons. Time: Twelve hours from the high bivouac.

28. North Mowich Face Icefall, 1970

This icefall, which forms the northern fringe of the Mowich Face, was first climbed by Jim Wickwire and Rob Schaller on June 26, 1970. The route ascends on and alongside the southern lobe of the North Mowich Face Icefall. There is some rock climbing at mid-face and in the top exit. Breakup and rock exposure suggests an early season and cold climb. Of historic interest is that a

The First Ascent of Liberty Ridge

Prior to the 1935 ascent of Liberty Ridge, Ome Daiber related that numerous climbers had a secret ambition to make its first ascent. Traveling light, Daiber's September 1935 team's equipment included 100 feet of climbing rope, 50 feet of thinner line, a Primus stove, a "blizzard" tent, willow wands, and food for four days. In the 1936 American Alpine Journal, Daiber wrote, "The closer we came to Willis Wall, the more we were thrilled by its ruggedness and the roaring avalanches!"

At one spot the party had cut a 30-foot staircase into glare ice to get out of a crevasse passage on the Carbon Glacier. Making a bivouac at 11,000 feet without sleeping bags, they cooked a supper of beef stew and cornmeal. Needless to say, they slept in all their clothing.

For late September, conditions at 11,000 feet were probably ideal: There was a frozen snow crust atop the glare ice and 6 inches of powdered snow atop the crust. Although the snow became deeper as they went higher, at times breaking through to their knees, they did not have to contend

portion of this icefall was descended by Wolf Bauer and Hans Grage after an attempt on Ptarmigan Ridge in September 1934.

Make the same approach as for the North Mowich Headwall. Traverse across the North Mowich Glacier to the base of a cleaver that separates the objective icefall from the North Mowich Headwall. On the first ascent the bergschrund was avoided by a steep leftward traverse (just below the cleaver's base). Climb the depression that parallels the lowest section of the icefall. Here several pitches on steep ice lead to a rock section that contains a 40-foot vertical pitch on sound rock. Climb two moderate rock pitches toward the snow and ice left and above the hourglass of the Headwall route.

Ascend the left edge of the broad néve slope, parallel to the latter route for 500 feet, then climb diagonally left through the upper icefall. Climb a 45-degree slope to the large cliff band forming the uppermost portion of Ptarmigan Ridge; take a gully to a final steep 30-foot rock pitch (class 5) that exits onto the néve slopes at 12,700 feet. Grade IV; bring ice screws and rock pitons. Time: Nine hours on the face.

Approach variation: From Ptarmigan Ridge.

with cutting steps, the practice of the times. Jubilant at the final crevasse problem, and certain they would now be victorious, Jim Borrow and Arnie Campbell threw Daiber across the crevasse by a one-leg pick-up and toss.

With this extraordinary climb in mind, we often ask, "Why don't climbers go light on technical routes such as Ptarmigan Ridge, Curtis Ridge, Sunset Ridge, the Mowich Face, and even the easier Success Cleaver?" Take a light tent or bivouac sack for each climber and some freeze-dried food to cook on the stove. Forget the wands (they litter one-way routes); bring a good compass. Go light and move along. Get to the summit and get off! If the weather is good, go for it. If it looks shaky, turn back. You don't see competent climbers doing Mont Blanc with 30- or 40-pound packs, then camping up high when they become fatigued (and perhaps getting rescued). If Daiber and his gallant gang could tough out a few frigid September nights on Rainier, why can't you? Years later, you'll fondly recall the shivering night far more than the night spent in the comfort-zone camp!

Karen Trank enjoys a spacious camp at 12,000 feet at the crest of Ptarmigan Ridge/North Mowich Face Icefall before tackling the steep water ice of the North Mowich Face Icefall in the morning. *(Alex Van Steen)*

Ptarmigan to Liberty Ridge

When the British navigator Capt. George Vancouver entered Puget Sound in 1792, the forbidding northwest flank of Mount Rainier was the first to come into view. If broken pieces of the grand Liberty Cap Glacier had been floating in the entrance waters, the skilled navigator might have been deterred from extending his exploration.

Despite this glacier's savage icecliffs, aspiring mountaineers came to this flank before the turn of the century. The western cirque of the spectacular and crevassed Carbon Glacier is a consequence of great erosive powers that have carved a vast hollow between the protruding Ptarmigan and Liberty ridges. Incessant glacier hollowing has honed Liberty Ridge into a strikingly linear and aesthetic precipitous cleaver, presenting a conspicuous contrast to the beetling eminence of Ptarmigan Ridge.

29. Ptarmigan Ridge

Possibly Mount Rainier's most impressive spur is Ptarmigan Ridge. It is the northwestern feature of the volcano, rising in a series of rocky, icy cliffs above the deep canyons of the North Mowich Glacier on the west and the broad surface of the Russell Glacier on the east. At 10,500 feet Ptarmigan Ridge forms a sheer face that features the 300-foot icecliff of the Liberty Cap Glacier (this cliff can easily be spotted from the Seattle–Tacoma area in clear weather). Above the rock bands and icecliffs near 12,500 feet, broad open glacier slopes lead south toward Liberty Cap.

Ptarmigan Ridge has the most vivid historic early attempts on Mount Rainier. For some reason, the 1884 party of J. Warner Fobes, George James, and Richard O. Wells ascended to possibly 10,000 feet on August 16. They halted abruptly at this location, perhaps the looming icecliffs having a bit to do with this. Fortunately, they had the good sense to backtrack and instead climb the Winthrop. In 1905 Lee Pickett of Bellingham claimed to have climbed Ptarmigan Ridge with one companion, an adventure accepted no more than flying saucer tales. However, in 1912 the very experienced alpinist Dora Keen (known for her Peruvian and Alaskan successes), with two others, attempted the route. She apparently reached 9,500 feet, but was halted by a sick companion, and another time by the wind.

Climbing tactics and philosophies have changed through time. In the 1930s there was a prevailing belief that September was the ideal period to climb Mount Rainier's northern technical routes (solid ice was preferable to avalanches of loose snow). In late summer 1933, Hans Grage, J. Wendell Trosper, and Jarvis Wallen climbed to about 11,000 feet to the right of the principal icecliff. They did some step-cutting, and climbed to the limit of their daylight. In 1934 Grage and Wolf Bauer made two attempts, getting to 12,500 feet (beyond nearly all difficulties). They ran out of time and did not wish to bivouac. With the mystery of the route solved, Bauer and Jack Hossack made the entire climb on September 7 and 8, 1935. They spent an

Opposite: Willis Wall, Liberty Ridge, and Liberty Wall *(Ed Cooper)*

Liberty Cap

Ptarmigan Ridge

Liberty Cap Glacier

1956

1968

Liberty Wall

1971

1955

1955

1935

Thumb Rock

Liberty Ridge

1976

1963

1965

1978

buttress

band

Traverse of Angels

1961

1970

frosty cliff

gray buttress

Willis Wall

1971

1965

Curtis Ridge

buttress

1974

boulder field cliff

1963

1971

1962

Carbon Glacier

incredible twelve hours cutting steps on ice and verglás. Amazingly, Ptarmigan Ridge was not climbed again for 24 years: In 1959 Gene and Bill Prater took the lower principal snow and ice slope, actually a variation of the 1935 route but now used by almost all parties.

A climber stands above high camp at the base of Ptarmigan Ridge. *(Don Goodman)*

The principal difficulties of the route lie between 10,500 feet and 12,500 feet, where it is not sheltered from rockfall, and where hard ice can slow a party (and rockfall perhaps speed it up). It is smart to make the climb during optimal temperature and snow conditions.

Procedure

The usual approach is by the road to Mowich Lake (via Buckley on SR 410, then through Carbonado on SR 165). Then hike about 3 miles to Spray Park. Leave the trail near 6,400 feet and gradually ascend parkland, lava, and snow slopes on a southwest bearing. Most parties cross the saddle between Echo and Observation Rocks, but there is wide latitude for route choice here. Then keep near the right (west) edge of the Russell Glacier (or follow pumice crests if the snow is soft). A steeper slope leads to Point 10,310 feet. One can make a high camp just below this point (some water is available in midsummer), or follow the crumbling narrow crest to a small col at 10,200 feet (keep east of the crest at the high

Opposite: The last steep slope high on Ptarmigan Ridge *(Alex Bertulis)*

Approaching the magnificent cirque at the head of the Carbon Glacier *(Dan Goering)*

Dan Davis above the last crevasse problem as the party weaves its way toward the summit snow dome
(Tom Stewart)

point). There is campsite space here, and one can look directly at the Liberty Cap
Icecliff not far above. Any falling ice will not strike the campsite, but it sometimes
cascades onto the slopes to the west.

From the narrow crest or the col, traverse west and downward to the edge of the
North Mowich Glacier. Cross ice litter hurriedly, then head for the bergschrund.
This has been an easy crossing; now make a long leftward ascent up the 45-degree
snow and ice slope to the large rock band heading it. Cross a minor spur, then

traverse closely beneath the rock cliff (this section will likely be icy after June). Rock protection is possible here. Climb a steep and shallow snow-ice apron to the final rock buttress at 12,000 feet. Note that there is an excellent tent campsite just right at the small notch near the apron. Traverse left under the buttress for some three leads to a steep ice chute at the edge of the Liberty Cap Glacier.

Climb the chute (one pitch) on the east of the buttress, then climb leftward through the crevasse–sérac area to an easier gradient higher. Changing conditions may make climbing upward, not left, the best choice. Keep near the crest of upper Ptarmigan Ridge and turn crevasses on the right. The ridge broadens, then merges with Sunset Ridge at 13,400 feet. Continue on or near the crest to Liberty Cap. Grade IV; bring ice screws and some rock protection; slings for rock horns may be particularly useful for the traverse of the rock band heading the initial slopes. Time: Seven to twelve hours from high camp.

Most parties descend the Emmons Glacier. The Disappointment Cleaver and Ingraham Glacier routes are other descent options.

Ascent variation via 1935 route of the first ascent: Climb close to the western base of the Liberty Cap Glacier icecliff, then through a chute in the first rock band; this face may be solid ice.

Bypass a large rock step via the ice slope to its west to join the now-normal route below the final rock buttress. Changing conditions now make this route less desirable and more vulnerable to objective hazard than the normal route.

Ascent variation (minor) via 1969 traverse: Climbed by Jim Wickwire and Rob Schaller in August 1969.

Where the normal route is forced left by the major rock band heading the principal ice slope, make an eastward traverse past the snow-ice apron and beneath the two easternmost rock cliffs. From a belay recess at the edge of the Liberty Cap Glacier climb a 55-degree slope.

Ascent variation via ice chute at 12,000 feet: Climb the ice chute near 12,000 feet, then traverse right on slabby rock under the icecliff to the true crest of Ptarmigan Ridge. Icefall conditions will govern difficulty. Above, continuous snow and ice lead to easier slopes.

Ascent variation via 1934 attempt: This is the line of the 1934 attempt. From the base of the final rock buttress, climb the snow-ice ramp on its west to a minor notch in the rock at its head. Then traverse snow (some rock rubble in late summer) above the upper edge of the Mowich Face. A narrow rock gully cuts into the band above. Exit to the upper glacier per the short but solid

A Dr. Science Question

Why is the sky usually a deeper blue at higher altitudes?

As we ascend, we leave much of the atmosphere below us. Also, the air is much cleaner at higher altitudes, since smoke, pollution, and water droplets are more concentrated in the lowermost levels of the atmosphere. By the time we reach 15,000 feet (slightly higher than Rainier), half the mass of the atmosphere and more than ninety percent of the contaminants are below us. Less air and fewer particles above mean that less incoming sunlight is scattered (i.e., reflected) by air molecules. With less scattered sunlight, the high-altitude sky is a much darker blue. If a mountain summit was 50,000 feet high, the daytime sky would be so dark that stars would appear.

Climbers far above Thumb Rock on Liberty Ridge *(Dan Goering)*

rock pitch of the North Mowich Face Icefall route. In September 1995, author Van Steen climbed this gully and found difficult and awkward water ice here (using ice screws to establish a belay in a protected alcove at the bottom left-hand side of the gully and one screw for the lower portion of the lead).

30. Ptarmigan Ridge–Liberty Cap Glacier, 1956

This route could be considered a separate one from Ptarmigan Ridge, or at least a major variation. Much of the route is the same, except that it traverses beneath the principal hanging icecliff of the Liberty Cap Glacier (one that can be seen as far away as Seattle). Conditions should be ideal to attempt this route and a certain pace should be kept under the icecliff. Changing conditions may alter portions of this route and its exit ramp. There are numerous theories regarding the best time to cross beneath such a large section of ice; certainly warm temperatures are not ideal, but ice can drop off any time just from glacier pressure and movement. The route's first ascent was made by John Rupley, Fred Beckey, and Herb Staley on August 4, 1956.

From the Ptarmigan Ridge high camp, ascend to the base of the great icecliff (near 11,000 feet). Make a left-hand diagonal traverse; some steep glazed rock may exist here. The sloping ramp will steepen (one may want ice screw protection). The 1956 party moved around a narrowing corner, did a 20-foot step to a ledge, then traversed steeply to a broad névé slope. A curved ice ramp permitted a cutback through the cliff to the upper glacier's surface. This ramp may or may not exist in the same conditions today. Continue per Ptarmigan Ridge. Grade III or IV; bring ice

Topping out on Liberty
Ridge can be a
challenging
undertaking, often
requiring lengthy
traverses to avoid the
upper crevasses or
steep direct lines.
(Dan Goering)

screws. Time: Ten hours from high camp to the crater rim. Descent note: The 1956 party found friends to carry down their high-camp gear and so were able to climb lighter and make a descent by Disappointment Cleaver.

31. Liberty Wall–Liberty Cap Glacier, 1968

The first ascent was made by Paul Myhre, Don Jones, and Roger Oborn on June 30, 1968. Approach this objective as for Liberty Ridge or from Spray Park, then ascend the glacier ramp between the Russell and Carbon Glaciers. Climb to the large bergschrund at the western head of the Carbon Glacier, then ascend the Liberty Wall slope. A portion of the climb is a long, continuous rib. An ice slope and rock bands offer a mixed route up a ramp that bears onto the Liberty Cap Glacier. The route has obvious objective dangers. Grade IV; bring ice screws and rock pitons. Time: Six hours from an 8,300-foot camp on the Carbon's edge to 12,300 feet on the Liberty Cap Glacier.

32. Liberty Wall Direct, 1971

This technical and perhaps hazardous route is east of the 1968 route, near the highest part of the headwall west of Liberty Ridge. The headwall icecliff is 150 to 250 feet high. The first ascent was made by Rainier Mountaineering guides Dusan Jagersky and Gary Isaacs on September 19 and 20, 1971.

On the 1971 climb, the team went from the Curtis Ridge high camp near 7,500 feet to the bergschrund at the base of an avalanche chute. Beware here, or bear left

Climbers move up excellent snow high on Mount Rainier's Liberty Ridge. *(Dan Goering)*

to safety. Keep just right of a broken-up ice ridge. A 45-degree slope continues to some solid rock bands. At the icecliff, one lead of hard climbing (ten ice screws) took the team to 45-degree slopes bearing toward Liberty Cap. The 1971 party made a bivouac in a crevasse under the top of the cap. Grade IV or V; bring ice screws and rock pitons. Time: Thirteen hours on the face.

33. Liberty Ridge, 1935

The distinct profile of Liberty Ridge, set amidst the headwall of the upper Carbon Glacier, gives this protrusion on Mount Rainier a remarkably pure line. Perhaps because the ridge knifes through the icecliffs atop Willis Wall, it takes on a classic character that makes the route the most popular of the technical ways to the summit. The true base of Liberty Ridge is about 8,000 feet, nearly 1,000 feet lower than the bergschrunds on adjacent Willis and Liberty Walls. The ridge ascends at a constant angle to about 13,100 feet, making it the volcano's steepest major cleaver.

The coveted route was first climbed by Ome Daiber, Arnie Campbell, and Jim Borrow on September 29 and 30, 1935. The ascent was done under very icy conditions, as one should anticipate in fall. The party had to bivouac at 11,000 feet and again on the summit.

Today, Liberty Ridge is generally climbed from May to July. Depletion of snowcover on the route will expose more rock and increase the chances of stonefall. A major disadvantage of an early season climb is that soft snow will probably be encountered on the fairly long approach, but don't discount the possibility of avalanches on Liberty Ridge's 35- to 45-degree slopes. Late-season climbs may be hindered by difficult navigation across the Winthrop and Carbon Glaciers. High camps or bivouacs are usually made at a small saddle at Thumb Rock (10,775 feet), where there is space for several tents. Occasionally parties camp on Curtis Ridge at 7,500 feet (on the Carbon's edge), then either make a break for the summit or take an additional day, making the second camp at Thumb Rock.

Do not push your luck on this long, sustained climb unless the weather is very good. The upper portion of Liberty Ridge and the continuation to Liberty Cap is a bad place to be in a whiteout or in stormy weather. There have been both tragedies and rescues because climbers were caught high on the route in poor conditions. In uncertain conditions, it is best to turn back low on the route and make a future attempt.

What You Need to Know About Radiative Exchanges

As Dr. Science of Canada explained in a recent newsletter, clouds are a quite effective emitter of long-wave radiation. You may have been informed that clouds "reflect" the earth's heat back to the earth at night, but this is patently a falsehood.

The presence of clouds increases the input of infrared radiation at the earth's surface. A famous (but possibly obscure to the climber) physical law states that the emissivity of any surface must equal its absorbtivity. Therefore, it follows that clouds absorb and re-radiate longwave radiation, rather than reflect it. Clouds above Mount Rainier at night keep temperatures warmer by radiating more energy to the surface than does the night sky. An increased radiation from a cloud blanket is enough to cause warmer surface temperatures. A campsite under a tree or even a canopy will be warmer than one directly under a very cold sky. But a cloud blanket will not give

Procedure

There are two approaches used to access Liberty Ridge: (1) From the White River Campground, through Glacier Basin, and over St. Elmo Pass, and (2) from the Carbon River Entrance and a hike to the eastern edge of the Carbon Glacier.

For the first approach, drive through Enumclaw from Seattle or Tacoma, following SR 410 for 38 miles from Enumclaw to the White River Entrance. Get a climbing permit here.

Drive in to the White River Campground (5 miles on the park road) and get ready to hike after you have found a parking spot at the trailhead (4,350 feet). Hike 3½ miles to the lower portion of Glacier Basin (there are campgrounds here). From the basin near 5,900 feet, take the climber's trail to 7,400-foot St. Elmo Pass. Now cross the Winthrop Glacier near the 7,500-foot-level to reach the broad slope of lower Curtis Ridge (ample camping space here), then drop to about 7,000 feet for easy access to the Carbon Glacier. Time: Allow the better part of a day to reach this location. If the party is well acclimatized, a campsite here is a good choice for a quicker ascent and lighter packs (as done by Yvon Chouinard, Fred Beckey, Dan Davis, Stan Shepard, and Eric Bjornstad on July 12, 1961).

Now descend onto the Carbon Glacier at about 6,900 feet. The descent is short, but can be loose if snow is melted. Ascend the crevassed Carbon to the base of Liberty Ridge. Most parties climb toward Willis Wall, taking the easiest line through crevasses and glacier breakups, then bear west around the crevasse mazes. It may save time to climb slightly higher, then make a traversing descent to the toe of the objective ridge.

The other approach is from Buckley (near SR 410 between Puyallup and Enumclaw). Drive on SR 165 to Carbonado and the Carbon River Entrance. The road end (2,300 feet) is 5 miles beyond (check with park headquarters to verify if the road is open to cars). Hike to Moraine Park and Mystic Lake (5,700 feet, just over 8 miles), then leave the trail just west of the lake to access the edge of the Carbon Glacier. Ascend easy glacier slopes and eventually get into the crevassed area of the upper glacier to reach the toe of Liberty Ridge. This approach can take one to one and a half days.

Most parties attain the lower crest of the objective ridge from the east flank at several hundred feet above its base (snow may provide an entry ramp but be prepared for a spooky bergschrund crossing if you are attempting a late-season climb) and make a moderately steep (loose dirt in late season) traverse to a position slightly west of the crest. Ascend the right flank of the ridge to the saddle above Thumb Rock.

There are three ways (all of about the same steepness and difficulty) to get up the next section—a rock step. Most parties climb rightward on néve or ice to the narrow gully that breaks the step, then ascend the gully. The other options are to keep either right (Dave Mahre's 1955 west-flank route) or left of the rock step.

Continue upward to reach the ridge crest and in some distance cross slightly leftward and ascend the slope to the top of the formation known as the Black Pyramid. Continue the moderately steep ascent until Liberty Ridge merges with the edge of the Liberty Cap Glacier. Then climb westward over a bergschrund (or bypass it if possible) to get around the upper icecliffs for the final glacier ascent (now easy) to Liberty Cap. This traverse west may be farther than at first expected.

Grade III or IV, depending upon conditions. Take ice screws and perhaps two pickets. Helmets are highly recommended on this route. Time: Seven to nine hours from Thumb Rock to Liberty Cap.

Descent: Nearly all parties descend the Emmons–Winthrop Glacier route. Be especially careful not to descend too soon onto the quickly steepening Winthrop. Several accidents and fatalities can be traced back to a route-finding error here.

you as much warmth as a woolen blanket, and a down sleeping bag is far superior to wool (and weighs less). If you ever feel sorry for past climbers burdened by heavy sleeping gear, think of the early Mount Rainier and Alaskan climbs, where alpinists carried heavy woolen blankets, heavy woolen Union suits, and perhaps wolfskin robes. Today, one can sleep blissfully, or closely against someone in this state, with less weight involved than in the good old days of 1896.

(Note: Credit for the above is due Trivial Fact #17161, Avalanche Echoes, *of the Alpine Club of Canada, November 1998.)*

Willis Wall

The distinguished geologist and professor Bailey Willis likely never thought anyone would climb the great northern face of Mount Rainier named in his honor. The wall rises some 3,600 feet at the head of the Carbon Glacier in a sweeping 45-degree face of lava and rock-strewn ice. Avalanches add to its character; these may come from the slope surface, along with falling rock, or from the 300-foot icecliffs at the rim of the summit dome. These cliffs have one exit ramp between Liberty Ridge and Curtis Ridge.

Willis Wall's three incomplete spur ribs, while protruding slightly above the general slope, offer little protection from objective hazards. There is a constant threat; day and night, vast ice avalanches have littered the glacier cirque.

While most avalanches follow couloirs parallel to ribs, débris can spill over the ribs. Without question, both Liberty and Curtis ridges are safer climbs.

Optimum conditions for ascent are ample consolidated snow surface and well-frozen (cold) conditions. Five routes (with variations) have been climbed on Willis Wall, and another on its eastern flank to the base of Curtis Ridge. The first climb (1961) generally followed the line of the most westerly of the spur ribs; the second route (1963) took the eastern of the ribs, and the third route (1965) the central rib.

No matter what route taken, the best advice is to get a calorie charge before crossing the bergschrund, do one or more "Hail Marys," and keep moving until you reach the summit dome rim. Perhaps there has been a special blessing to climbers, for the wall itself has not witnessed a tragedy.

34. Thermogenesis, 1978

This steep route takes a 55-degree couloir right of the West Rib and was first climbed by Steve Doty, Jerome Eberharter, and Jon Olson on May 20, 1978. This party encountered a variety of conditions, ranging from firm snow to water ice and loose rock. They took seven hours to the end of the couloir at 12,500 feet from a crevasse bivouac at 10,000 feet. As with other routes on the wall, there is some hazard.

Grade IV or V; bring ice screws and rock pitons.

35. Willis Wall, West Rib (Damocles Rib or Brumal Buttress), 1961

The upper portion of this distinct rib flattens into a broad face some 500 feet below the summit icecliff. There may be some hazard protection where the rib protrudes. On Charlie Bell's solo climb during June 11 and 12, 1961, he had to angle westward to upper Liberty Ridge. Bell made another climb in 1962, crossing the bergschrund near the top of Liberty Ridge. Alex Bertulis and Jim Wickwire made another ascent (February 10 and 11, 1970) and climbed to the base of the highest icecliff; then they angled across to upper Liberty Ridge. The complete rib and icecliff was not climbed in its entirety until the Boley–Lewis ascent of 1976 (see variation).

Mount Rainier: Northeast Quadrant
Routes 36–44

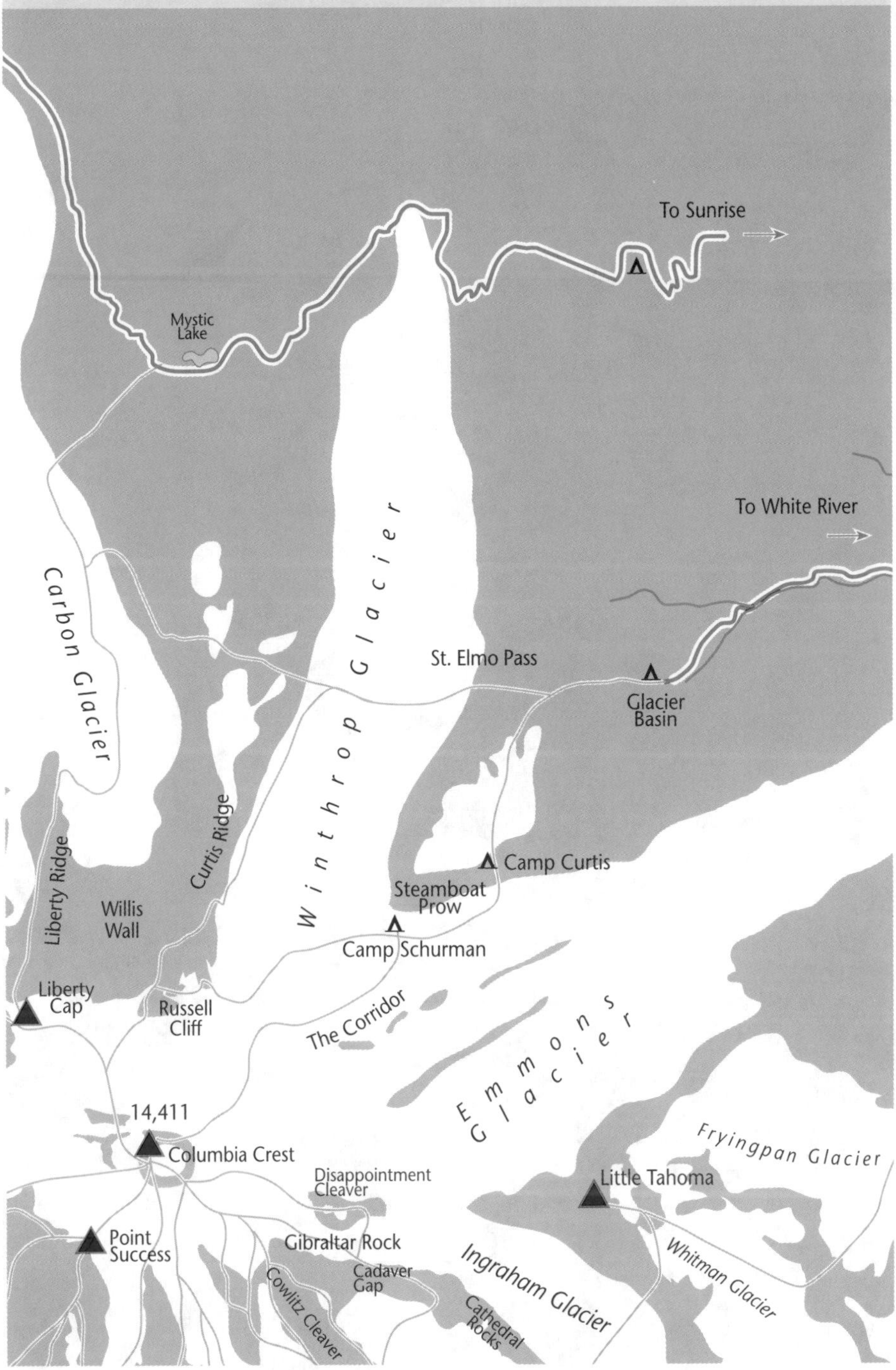

To Sunrise

Mystic
Lake

To White River

Carbon Glacier

Winthrop Glacier

St. Elmo Pass

Glacier
Basin

Curtis Ridge

Liberty Ridge

Willis
Wall

Camp Curtis

Steamboat
Prow

Camp Schurman

Liberty
Cap

Russell
Cliff

The Corridor

Emmons
Glacier

Fryingpan Glacier

14,411

Columbia Crest

Disappointment
Cleaver

Little Tahoma

Point
Success

Gibraltar Rock

Cadaver
Gap

Ingraham Glacier

Whitman Glacier

Cowlitz Cleaver

Cathedral
Rocks

View up toward a steep rock band on the West Rib of Willis Wall in February 1970 *(Alex Bertulis)*

Make the same approach as for Liberty Ridge, but bear to the upper right portion of the glacier cirque. Cross the bergschrund where most feasible and make a direct ascent. After climbing the lower portion of the icefield, work over several rock bands and a difficult 75-foot cliff (a crux). Then follow the crest of the buttress. Most rock steps can be avoided by traversing around on the left. Where the buttress terminates into a steep snow slope bearing to the final rock bands below the icecliff, a snow terrace goes to the cliff's corner. Make a difficult and steep traverse (probably ice) to upper Liberty Ridge. Grade IV or V; bring ice screws and a rock piton selection. Time: Ten to twelve hours to Liberty Cap.

Ascent variation, upper icecliff: A complete ascent via the West Rib was made by Tomas Boley and Jack Lewis on February 7, 1976. The party climbed from a saddle beneath the icecliff up "salt and pepper" rock bands to the cliff. Two steepish pitches of ice were done on a leftward slant through the cliff. Climbing time was ten to twelve hours. Bring ice screws and possibly pickets. Grade IV or V.

Opposite: View of the East Rib of the Willis Wall *(Alex Van Steen)*

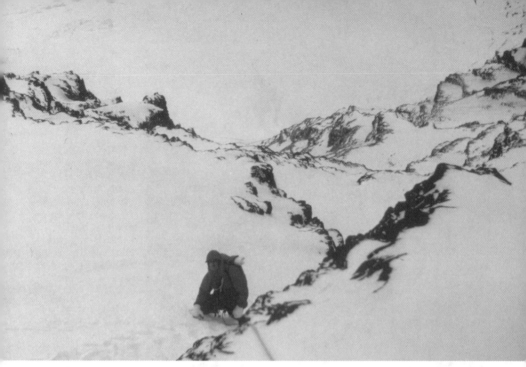

Looking steeply down the West Rib high on Willis Wall *(Alex Bertulis)*

36. Willis Wall, Central Rib (Agricola Rib), 1965

This rib, with a slightly leftward bearing, is located about midway between Liberty and Curtis Ridges. Where the Central Rib ends to merge into the open snow and ice, the first ascent party followed the East Rib route, but made a different exit from the summit icecap arm. They reported that cramponing was generally good (a few steps were cut) but some rock areas were covered with verglás.

The first ascent was made by Dean Caldwell and Paul Dix on June 20, 1965, and the next climb was by Ed Boulton and Jim Wickwire on May 12 and 13, 1971.

Cross the bergschrund after making the Liberty Ridge approach and climb onto snow immediately east of the rib's terminus. Climb directly to the crest (rockfall experienced here). Above are four arching bands of rock that cross the rib; cross them left of the rib crest.

The second ascent party crossed the bergschrund on the west of the rib's terminal and thereby avoided the arches by climbing on continuous snow near the rib's crest. After the fourth arch, climb rightward on a snow slope for several hundred feet to where it is feasible to traverse left on a crumbling ledge to the top of short cliffs. Now climb a gray buttress and around its left side on snow, then gain its top. Climb a short, narrow snow-ice chute above and slightly left, then traverse right to slabby rock. Climb to a very steep "frosty cliff" of snow and rock, then make a difficult leftward bypass traverse on rock (class 5) for some 40 feet. Mixed ground continues to the juncture of the route with the East Rib.

There are ascent options at this point. Now climb to the ice terrace and summit exit as for the East Rib route description. (The first Central Rib party varied at the final ice wall by climbing into a crevasse then chimneying out of it.)

The route is Grade IV or V; take ice screws and rock pitons. Time: One or two days.

Ascent variation: By Dusan Jagersky and Greg Markov in May 1973. From near midway on the rib this team made an ascending traverse to the eastern flank of Willis Wall to the final pitches of Curtis Ridge.

37. Willis Wall, East Rib (Prometheus Rib), 1963

This rib is the most protected from objective dangers of the three ribs on Willis Wall, although the lower portion has potential hazards. The rib has a leftward trend and flattens into the Wall at about two-thirds of the distance to the icecap; here a traverse has been made to the Central Rib. At some 1,500 feet higher, the only break in the icecap is climbed via a terrace-ramp to the summit glacier slopes. The route's first ascent was made by the very experienced team of Dave Mahre, Fred Dunham, Jim Wickwire, and Donald N. Anderson on June 8, 1963.

Make the same approach as for other Willis Wall routes (the Liberty Ridge approach), then cross the left end of the bergschrund—or where possible. Take a rightward arc to reach the rib's crest. Continue up to its end at a buttress some 1,500 feet up the wall (there is steep and poor rock near the completion of this section). Now climb to the head of a small ridge and make a rising right traverse on the sloping snow-ice band to the central avalanche couloir (there may be thin ice over rock). Cross to another short ridge, then ascend a trough on its right; here join the Central Rib.

Climb several leads to some short rock bands at the base of the summit icecliff. Begin a rock pitch some 60 feet left of a conglomerate cliff with a snow ledge atop. Climb a rotten ledge up and right to a nasty section (frozen mud with large embedded rocks). Traverse left steeply and then climb a 20-foot solid rock wall (angle piton protection). From the first and second bands begin the "traverse of the angels." Turn right and in a narrowing 40 feet make an unprotected crawl under a roof. Then climb a snow ramp. At 200 feet there is a thermal moat under a rock band (a possible bivouac site). Now climb moderate slopes rightward, then through a gap behind a grouping of séracs formed by a split in the icecap. Traverse glacier slopes westward just below the final bergschrund until it ends, then climb directly left and upward to the crater rim.

Grade V; take ice screws and rock pitons. Time: One to two days. Note that changing conditions may provide different problems and situations from that of the early routes.

Ascent variation: A major variation of the East Rib route was done on a climb by Jim Wickwire and Dusan Jagersky. On March 24, 1974 this highly skilled pair made a rapid ascent, taking new ground for some 70 percent of the way, only repeating the 1963 route for several hundred feet just below the traverse made earlier to reach the upper rib. Wickwire recalls being in the middle of the couloir between the East and Central Ribs, where they spent "a couple of hours" of what could be understated as "tension." Of his four Willis Wall climbs, the 1974 ascent was his most enjoyable.

Ascent variation: By Lee Nelson and Rob Schaller on June 15 and 16, 1971. This party reported considerable difficult water ice on the route. They made a leftward traverse of 400 feet to join the Curtis Ridge route just beneath the final exit gullies.

38. Willis Wall, East Face, 1962

This route climbs the very eastern flank of Willis Wall and then merges into the upper portion of Curtis Ridge at about 12,500 feet. The first ascent was made by Ed Cooper and Mike Swayne on June 26, 1962; the party made a bivouac on the upper Carbon Glacier and then spent eight hours on the final ascent.

Approach as for Liberty Ridge and continue to the upper eastern section of the glacier headwall. Cross the bergschrund where it curves left from Willis Wall, then climb the steep snow slope on the Curtis Ridge flank. Ascend broken rock and snow to a key ramp, then take it right on a long traverse to bypass cliffs. Near the end of the ramp climb the long rock band above a boulder field-cliff to reach the ice slope higher (very loose rock). Then climb a mix of snow and rock until the slope eases to the ice crowning upper Curtis Ridge.

Grade IV; take ice screws and possibly some rock pitons.

Climb Rainier in a Day?!

Sure, it's possible, and in fact most of Rainier's major routes have been climbed in a day (twenty-four hours or less, from car to car). What does it take to get started? First of all, potential one-day climbers should be well trained and have solid snow and glacier skills. If it's your first "one-dayer," choose an easier and shorter route, and time your ascent so you avoid daytime heat and the crowds. Take the usual Rainier summit gear, plus some extra food and water to keep your team fueled. A climb rate (including stops) of 1,000 feet per hour over the length of the ascent is an "average" speed; much slower than that might warrant a turn-around short of the summit, depending on your route. Good luck!

Jason Edwards

A climber traverses the open slopes beneath the final rock butress on Ptarmigan Ridge, at about 12,000 feet. *(Dan Davis)*

Curtis Ridge to Emmons Glacier

The northern flank of Mount Rainier is so dominated by the sprawling mass of the combined Emmons and Winthrop Glaciers that the flanking steep rock spur known as Curtis Ridge is barely noticeable at first sight. When early mountaineers approached this flank, it was apparent that this spur would not be an appealing ascent. Although heavily crevassed, the two combined glaciers presented a far more reasonable route to the summit dome.

These glaciers continually pour milky-colored water into the White River, the volcano's largest stream. The Emmons, which is the largest body of glacial ice in the Cascade Range, has behaved variably in the past four centuries. Several times the glacier was broader and thicker, and formed high lateral moraines down valley (nine moraines have been dated since the year 1596). After a half century of progressive stagnation, the Emmons began an advancing front in 1953, and for nearly twenty years ice above the river outlet thickened. Climatic warming, however, has continued the general recessive trend.

Two climbers at the base of the rock thumb, just past the rappel of Point 10,284 feet, which starts the technical climbing *(Tom Stewart)*

Opposite: Mount Rainier from the northeast
(USGS, courtesy Geophysical Institute, University of Alaska Fairbanks)

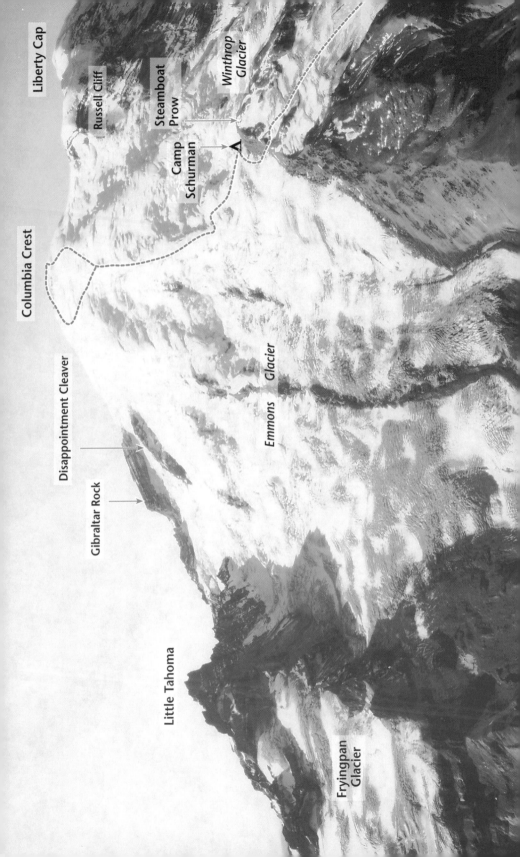

Liberty Cap

Russell Cliff

Steamboat Prow

Winthrop Glacier

Camp Schurman

Columbia Crest

Disappointment Cleaver

Emmons Glacier

Gibraltar Rock

Little Tahoma

Fryingpan Glacier

39. Curtis Ridge, 1957

Curtis Ridge is the commanding spur on Mount Rainier's northern face that separates Willis Wall from the sprawling Winthrop Glacier. While Curtis Ridge has prominence, it is not as easily distinguished as some of the other spurs on the volcano, such as Ptarmigan Ridge, Sunset Ridge, or Success Cleaver. Lower Curtis Ridge sweeps broadly to a prominent rock point at about 10,300 feet; here there is a level section, succeeded by a gap, then a series of vertical cliff bands separated by steep snow and loose rock.

Attempts on this ridge date back to the 1930s, but were hampered by problems of loose rock in overcoming a prominent 75-foot vertical step at about 10,800 feet and the anticipated danger of rockfall higher. This problem was finally solved on the first ascent in 1957.

The climb was made a week after a snowstorm, in cool temperatures; the loose area had not yet thawed so the party did not experience the anticipated rockfall. One should keep moving along on this climb, and it might be wise to avoid the direct aid sections and take bypass variations (1965 "Open Book" and 1969 variations), which are faster.

1957 original route: First done by Gene Prater and Marcel Schuster on July 21, 1957, with support from Bob McCall, Stan Butchart, and Herb Buller.

Approach from White River Campground, over St. Elmo Pass, and cross the Winthrop Glacier. A campsite can be found on Curtis Ridge at 8,500 feet (allow six to eight hours to here). From here ascend to the apex of gradual snow slopes at the 10,284-foot rock point shown on the map. There is another good camp platform about ten minutes below, on the north side. This is the last really comfortable site, but it is far from the climbing problems. Climb down and rappel 50 feet off of the southwest corner of the buttress point onto a steep snowfield on the west side of the ridge.

Ascend and traverse the snowfield to the narrow rock crest. Follow it to the giant rock thumb (a small drop-off near the end of the crest may require a jump or short rappel to snow on the west). Alternatively, the steep snowfield has been traversed on a rise for several leads, then an open snow slope climbed to the crest north of the thumb.

Skirt the thumb on its east via a bench at ridge level (possible bivouac here and also beyond the prow-gendarme on its west),

Traversing east around the "rock thumb" *(Tom Stewart)*

Crampons to Remember

Crampons were introduced in the Alps before 1870, although their usage was quite limited until 1914. A Briton, Oscar Eckenstein, made ten-point crampons in 1910, but the Brits, led by Alfred Mummery, were more interested in rock than ice. By the 1920s, when their usage became universal, crampons had become lighter and their design much improved. The French perfected crampon technique in the Alps (hence the term, "French technique").

In the 1930s the Austrians added two front points to crampons and welded a bar across the hinge to make them rigid. With such improvements, by the late 1930s many of the elusive and difficult icy north faces of the Alps were climbed. It is now almost universal to use twelve-point anodized steel crampons that cap boot welts, and with click-in heel levers.

Edmund T. Coleman, the British alpinist who lived in Victoria, British Columbia for some years, used crampons on Mount Baker in 1866 and 1868, and took them to Mount Rainier in

Mike Heath belays Gene Ohlson at the finish of the "Open Book" crux west of the original aid line on Curtis Ridge. *(Gary Glenn)*

or follow the prow, then make a short rappel on its west. This brings one to the small saddle beneath the 75-foot vertical step.

There are several ways to negotiate the step, but avoid going too far east. The original route is the aid crack about 100 feet west of the ridge. The rock can be quite rotten (up to four hours have been spent here). The second ascent party used about seven aid pitons, finding a block had fallen out to lengthen the overhang. Above the aid some loose, steep rock leads to a belay spot. The general line now follows open snow slopes just west of the crest to the base of the second major rock step. Traverse right some distance on a snow band until it narrows (at about 11,500 feet). Here about 50 feet of low-angle rock climbing with possible ice coating (middle class 5) gains access to the largest snowfield on Curtis Ridge.

Climb diagonally left across the snow slope to again reach the crest. Ascend to a final ice- or snow-filled exit gully east of the crest; at the mouth of the ice gully (12,500 feet) there may be a short pitch of sloping rock (class 5). Front pointing and two ice tools may be required in the 20-foot-wide gully. The gully's continuation (steep icy snow) exits to the crest of upper Curtis Ridge. Ascend the easy glacier ice toe to the summit.

Grade IV; class 5 and aid (note that any route or variation could become a Grade V).

1965 "Open Book" variation: First climbed by Dan Davis, Mark Fielding, Curtis Stout, and Don McPherson on May 30, 1965.

At the foot of the 75-foot vertical step angle up, right, on ice below the rock band for about 200 to 300 feet to a narrower part of the band where the rock looks both sounder and easier. Here is a shallow open book (vertical for about 10 feet, then rounding off). Use several pitons (angles to horizontals) or chocks for aid, then climb upward and left on slabs to a platform for a scramble to the original route.

1967 "Second Step" variation: First climbed by Tom Stewart, Mike Heath, Gary Glenn, Gene Ohlson, and Bruce Loughlin in June 1967.

From the base of the second rock step climb directly up a 100-foot gray rock pitch closely right of the true crest. (First part solid class 5, last part rubbly class 4.)

1969 variation: First climbed by Jim Wickwire, Del Young, and Ed Boulton on November 1 and 3, 1969.

This variation turns the first rock band some 200 feet west of the 1965 variation. Continue beyond the 1965 open book to where it is feasible to climb the band on broken rock (two slabs and a short class 3 pitch over the top of the band), then bear left and upward. This party turned the second step with ice climbing, using a frozen waterfall (difficult, three screws), which provided a quicker way than the rock pitch just to the left.

1870. These crampons, brought from Europe, were the first to be used in North America.

40. Western Russell Cliff, 1960

This reddish beetling crag is named for the renowned geologist Israel C. Russell, who made an early climb of the Winthrop Glacier.

Russell Cliff rises above the Winthrop Glacier's northern margin from about 11,000 feet to 13,400 feet. On the lower flanks (beneath Curtis Ridge) this cliff is very steep and loose. Higher, a shallow bowl is framed by Curtis Ridge on the right and a rock spur adjacent to the glacier. This provides an indentation and route access to upper Curtis Ridge. The first ascent was made by Dave Mahre, Gene Prater, Jim Kurtz, and Don Jones in July 1960.

From Camp Schurman at Steamboat Prow (see the Emmons–Winthrop Glacier route), climb up and across the Winthrop's trough between crevassed areas to about 11,000 feet. Then ascend the snow-ice below the shallow bowl. The route here traverses northerly and climbs a 600-foot snow slope, ending at the far right extension of the snowfield in the bowl. Follow a snow band north across the cliffs, then ascend a gully or break in the rock to the crest of Curtis Ridge at about 12,500 feet.

Grade II or III. Time: Ten hours from camp.

41. Central Russell Cliff, 1973

First ascent was made by Dean Bentley, Jim Springer, and John L. Thompson on July 8, 1973. From the bowl proceed directly up the snow face to three prominent rock bands. The 1973 party, as

well as subsequent parties, encountered unstable snow atop thin water ice at breaks through the bands. Traverse narrow snow ledges on the upper portion of the rock bands.

The final exit slopes above Russell Cliff are often very icy, or ice-covered with a thin veneer of snow. These slopes are affected by the same weather and wind patterns that often give this side of the mountain a midseason coating of ice.

Grade II or III. Bring ice screws and rock protection. Time: Eight hours from Camp Schurman to the summit.

A Serious Injury During Climbing Course Practice

Communications at park headquarters received a cellphone call concerning a fall during ice climbing practice on the Nisqually Glacier. The climber involved fell near the top of the climb shortly after placing his last ice screw. Due to soft conditions, all of his ice screws pulled out, resulting in a 40-foot fall.

A jet rescue helicopter met two park rangers at the helibase for what proved to be a difficult evacuation (the pilot was required to pull power while on one and a half skids as the injured climber was loaded into the ship). He was flown to a medical center in Seattle, where it was determined that his injuries included a compression fracture of vertebrae and a fractured hip.

The analysis printed in Accidents in North American Mountaineering *(edited by Jed*

Mike Lobosco and Alex Van Steen prepare for the steeper slopes of Russell Cliff above. *(Mike Hattrup)*

Opposite: Spectacular rock climbing through the "Second Step" variation on Curtis Ridge. The rock quickly turns to rubbly class 4, but is enjoyable and exposed here on the crest. *(Tom Stewart)*

Mike Hattrup clambers through large pieces of broken andesite, the mountain's signature rock quality. *(Mike Lobosco)*

42. Eastern Russell Cliff, 1974

A third route on Russell Cliff was done by Gene Prater and Dave and Chris Mahre in 1974. This party climbed the snow face through some minor rock bands just to the Winthrop side of the prominent rock buttress.

Grade II or III. Bring ice screws and rock protection. Time: Six to eight hours from Camp Schurman to the summit.

43. Emmons and Winthrop Glaciers, 1884

The combination of the Emmons and Winthrop Glaciers, a huge mass of glacier ice emanating from the summit icecap of Mount Rainier, is by far the largest on the mountain (and in the United States outside of Alaska). The combined upper portion of the two glaciers is divided by the great wedge of Steamboat Prow at about 9,500 feet. This immense wedge pushes the Winthrop westward and the Emmons eastward. The noted geologist Francois Matthes once wrote that the Prow parts these glaciers "like swift-flowing waters upon the dividing bow of a ship."

The Emmons, nearly 5 miles in length, is named for the geologist Samuel Emmons, who made the first glacier studies on Mount Rainier. The Winthrop is named in honor of the adventurer Theodore Winthrop, who authored a classic book, *The Canoe and the Saddle*, about his travels in the Pacific Northwest.

The first ascent of this glacier route was made by a completely inexperienced (and lucky) party from Snohomish, Washington. The three climbers who made the ascent on August 20, 1884 (the Reverend J. Warner Fobes, George James, and Richard O. Wells) were not really aware that Mount Rainier had ever been climbed. The next ascent (July 24, 1896) was by an experienced party, and one that was again not aware of the earlier ascent. This climb was a U.S. Geological Survey effort by Bailey Willis, George Otis Smith, Israel C. Russell, F. H. Ainsworth, and William D. Williams, to not only make the ascent but to conduct scientific investigations.

Procedure

From one of the Puget Sound area cities, drive to Enumclaw (the usual approach is SR 410 or SR 164). Then drive 38 miles to the White River Entrance and continue 5 miles to the White River campground. You must get a climbing permit at the ranger station.

Hike 3½ miles on the good trail along the Inter Fork of the White River to the lower portion of Glacier Basin. Some parties make their first camp here. Continue hiking up to the basin to access the lower portion of the Inter Glacier, near 7,000 feet. Ascend some 1,500 feet on this gentle but accident-prone glacier (icy slopes and hidden crevasses have fooled several parties). Most parties elect to stay near the center or right portion of the glacier.

Then angle toward the bare ridge on the southeast rim of the glacier at 9,000 feet. From the rock rim traverse a pumice slope eastward onto the edge of the Emmons, then ascend the glacier to the base of the Prow. Most climbing parties camp near the Camp Schurman hut (9,500 feet) at the base of the Prow, or tent-camp on Emmons Flats (9,800 feet, on the glacier). There are some 23 designated sites at Camp Curtis (8,200 feet) on the ridge at the western edge of the Inter Glacier, but these sites are usually avoided due to their exposure to the winds. Time: Allow six to eight hours from the road.

From the Prow, a long and smooth slope ("The Corridor") above and slightly left (east) is taken to near the 12,000-foot-level. Here the corridor fades and the glacier becomes more crevassed. Many variations on the broad glacier expanse are possible here. Most parties bear rightward to the final crevasse (bergschrund) of the Winthrop (near 13,000 feet), but some years the route is forced

Williamson and published annually by the American Alpine Club) states that the climber may not have realized the dubious nature of protection placed in glacial ice under warm summer conditions. Scraping away surface slush and using long screws is strongly recommended when leading glacial ice under such conditions. Mock leading (under the safeguard of a top rope) is probably much safer in these conditions. The preparedness and the risks taken by the helicopter pilot were related factors that in this case resulted in a rapid and safe rescue. It should be mentioned that this group was well-prepared, having their own litter (source: Mike Gauthier, Mount Rainier National Park).

east toward the Emmons Shoulder. The crucial part of the entire route is getting across this gap to reach the summit dome area. Then work into the broad saddle between Columbia Crest and Liberty Cap. Finally, bear leftward on the gradual slope to reach the crater rim, an often agonizing crawl.

Grade I or II. Time: Five to eight hours from Steamboat Prow.

A few reminders: This is really a magnificent glacier route on Mount Rainier, one without special difficulty and quite popular. The state of the glacier varies according to the year and the time of the year. As on any route to the summit, beware of poor weather and whiteouts. Keep slack out of the rope. Some of the crevasses are huge and may be hidden. Several accidents have occurred when snow bridges collapsed or when climbers walked blindly into crevasses in poor visibility. Sections of the Emmons Glacier are suprisingly hollow, dangerous, and unknown to most climbers traveling on the surface. Unfortunately, other accidents and fatalities have occurred when climbers slipped on ice in late season (usually on descent, when fatigue is a factor). Often, high winds surprise climbers, even experienced ones, and the hard ice can be terribly unforgiving.

Previous page: Ron Servine reflects on a satisfying climb while atop Steamboat Prow. *(Jason Edwards)*

Opposite: Tents near Camp Schurman in early evening *(Alex Van Steen)*

Overleaf: The difficulties of the upper Emmons route often lie in negotiating the final crevasses, which tend to push the route on long traverses to the east or west. *(Jason Edwards)*

Columbia Crest

East Crater

Ptarmigan Ridge

Camp Schurman

Steamboat Prow

Emmons Glacier

K's Spire

Northeast Face

Fryingpan Glacier

Gibraltar Rock

Little Tahoma

9,000' notch

Whitman Crest

Camp Muir

Cathedral Rocks

Ingraham Glacier

Whitman Glacier

Cowlitz Glacier

Ohanapecosh Glacier

Little Tahoma (11,138 feet)

The once-higher Mount Rainier volcano's eruptions, and erosion of its flanks, left standing an isolated, towering satellite, a remnant of high craggy rock between glaciers. As the dominant topographic feature on Mount Rainier's eastern flank, Little Tahoma forms an immense wedge between the Ingraham and Emmons Glaciers. Almost like ice pancakes, the opposite slope of Little Tahoma is adorned by the smaller Fryingpan and Ohanapecosh Glaciers.

Little Tahoma is formed of andesite lava flows that, as its bedding indicates, once formed part of the crest of the peak. But now it is an isolated, triangular formation, a jagged rock peak rising some 3,000 feet above its surrounding icefields.

The flanking glaciers are vigorously destroying the crumbling walls of this massive rock pyramid. To add to the destruction, volcanic steam vents and associated heat activity have altered its structure. One example of this type of destruction occurred in December 1963, when large rock slides on the peak's north face shed the débris of a weakened section over 4 miles down the Emmons Glacier. Geologists believe that air cushions buoyed the débris airborne, so that today masses of broken rock lie on the valley floor beyond the glacier terminus. Humanity was spared loss of life because this event occurred in midwinter, but the many great volcanic hazards of Mount Rainier are time bombs waiting their moment of glory. One only needs to recall that the Osceola Mudflow (which occurred some 5,800 years ago) created a path of devastation far beyond the city of Enumclaw.

Compared to a climb to the summit of Mount Rainier, Little Tahoma is a different type of experience, one without the committing glacier and altitude problems. Its alpine setting and superb location on the flanks of the parent volcano make Little Tahoma a popular climb. The first ascent was made by botanist and ranger J. B. Flett with Henry H. Garrison on August 29, 1894. Their route took them through Summerland and the normally used east shoulder.

Opposite: Mount Rainier from the east *(USGS, courtesy Geophysical Institute, University of Alaska Fairbanks)*

44. East Shoulder, 1894

This facet of Little Tahoma has the least gradient, the "sloping" side, which holds the Whitman Glacier like a cradle. It is the route used by virtually all parties, either from Summerland or from Paradise.

Procedure

Using the northern approach, drive via Enumclaw and SR 410 to the White River Entrance. The trail to 5,400-foot Summerland begins 3 miles from the entrance (3,900 feet), and is an easy 4⅕-mile hike. One can camp here or at a higher altitude; note that overnight camping permits are required.

Skirt rock cliffs to their right and then ascend southward on a rounded slope to 7,000-foot Meany Crest. You may see wandering goats in the neighborhood. One or more herds tend to wander about on various crests on this flank of Little Tahoma and eastward near Fryingpan Gap.

Then bear southwest (at 235 degrees true north) onto the Fryingpan Glacier near 7,500 feet. At 7,580 feet, angle west at 260 degrees on flat terrain. Ascend the glacier southwest to the 9,000-foot notch connecting Whitman Crest to Little Tahoma (this notch is west of the 9,364-foot high point on Whitman Crest). Note that in late summer this notch area can become icy.

Now traverse southwest around the first rock outcrop and then climb to the head of the Whitman Glacier (about 10,500 feet). Some loose rock slopes (or snow) lead through the snow gully on the left side of the crest to within about 200 feet of the summit. There is a potentially serious rockfall problem in the upper gully. Do not take a large party into the gully and do not enter it if others are above.

Then work left through a rock break (expect some crumbly stone). Ascend rightward to the crest and follow to a small notch; the rope is advised when crossing the exposed notch some 15 feet below the true summit point.

Erosion near the summit crest has made the ascent more dangerous. Most parties do not rope up except for this section, but one should use discretion everywhere.

Grade I. Time: Seven hours from Summerland.

A party climbing snow of Little Tahoma above the Fryingpan Glacier *(Don Goodman)*

UFO Sightings Began on Mount Rainier

The term "flying saucer" originated from a strange sighting of nine forms and a blue flash by pilot Kenneth Arnold while flying past Mount Rainier on June 24, 1947. The pilot was interviewed about his sighting of these peculiar luminescent objects by CBS newsman Edward R. Murrow some three years later. Such diverse UFOs, or "flying saucers," which may be optical mirages, haven't proven credible.

On an earth where supposedly intelligent life has suggested that the Milky Way is composed not of stars, but of snowballs, there have been numerous deceptive accounts of extraterrestrial life. Author Carl Sagan, in The Demon-Haunted World, *reminds us that the general public's understanding of these moving objects is that they resemble very large*

Ascents of Little Tahoma are becoming increasingly popular. Here a party is descending avalanche débris of an earlier slide. *(Don Goodman)*

Paradise approach variation: Be certain to bring a topographic map and compass if using this approach. From Paradise (5,420 feet) follow the Skyline Trail via Panorama Point and Pebble Creek to about 8,500 feet (below Anvil Rock). Then begin a traverse near 8,600 feet, crossing the Cowlitz Glacier to the 8,400-foot notch in Cathedral Rocks Ridge (be careful to keep above the crevasse field below that level). Make a slight descent to cross Cathedral Rocks and traverse directly across the Ingraham Glacier to attain a position below a prominent notch (about 8,900 feet) that leads to the Whitman Glacier. Ascend loose and down-sloping slabs to this notch, then ascend Whitman Glacier to join the Summerland route. Time: Nine to eleven hours from Paradise. Most parties will want to place a campsite en route.

45. Other Routes

Few climbers attempt any but the standard route. The south face, west ridge, north face, and northeast face have all been climbed, but are seldom done. All are climbs of technical difficulty and have a certain risk from rockfall. Needless to state, conditions should be optimum to reduce such risk.

South Face, 1991

From the Ingraham Glacier, ascend the central snow couloir on the south face to the base of its headwall. The headwall is bound on either side by shallow but distinctive ribs. The route has three pitches of moderately difficult rock that culminate at Little Tahoma's false summit.

First ascent by Jim Yoder and Kevin Buselmeier in June 1991. Grade IV, class 5.8; bring modern rock protection to 3 inches and a few pitons. Time: Eight hours from a camp low on Cathedral Rocks Ridge. This party used the Paradise approach and reported good rock quality—for Rainier.

and highly maneuverable Frisbees.

On the mountain, keeping an eye open for possible UFOs and blue flashes may be a good tactic to ease the monotony of plodding uphill, but watching for hidden crevasses is a superior plan to remain healthy.

Other Routes

A party scrambling the summit rock of Little Tahoma on a pleasant day *(Don Goodman)*

West Ridge, 1981

This excellent route features spectacular climbing, but it has poor rock and a high level of objective hazard. The first ascent party of Paul Cook and Matt Christensen (December 31, 1980 and January 1, 1981) had true winter conditions; nevertheless, they encountered rock- and icefall when forced to the south flank of the ridge.

From Camp Muir traverse the Ingraham Glacier to gain the ridge via a snow and ice chute (some rock climbing). On the ridge, traverse steep snow and ice slopes on the north face just below the crest (one rappel in this section). Near midpoint of the ridge, vertical rock walls force one to the crest. A ramp leads onto the south face for over one pitch. Climb a 40-foot vertical rock wall to gain a snow patch below the first of two large steep rock steps. Gain the ridge crest by this snow. Now climb the steep step in two or more fairly easy leads (good rock). Rappel from the top of the step to a snowfield at the base of the last rock step (a bivouac can be made here).

The final rock step includes four difficult and serious leads. First traverse right on a ramp from the notch at the head of the snowfield. The crux move here could be barely protected with a piton for 40 feet (poor rock and serious runout). From a good belay climb solid class 5.6 rock. Then bear right to a snowpatch on the south face; climb diagonally left to the crest on a snow and rock ramp. From the ridge crest at the ramp's end, climb a vertical wall (class 5.7) for 80 feet to the top of the second step. A short rappel and one difficult rock pitch leads along the very narrow ridge to the summit.

Grade V; class 5.7. The first ascent party belayed on 18 pitches, placing 25 pitons or chocks and three ice screws. Three 75-foot rappels were made. Crampons were worn on all but two pitches.

North Face, 1959 and 1979

This steep face heads directly above the Emmons Glacier; the route crosses over the Northeast Face route and finishes on the East Shoulder in its final portion. First ascent by Gene Prater and Dave Mahre in June 1959.

Hike to the gap in the northern cleaver of Little Tahoma just above K's Spire (possible campsite here). Descend onto the Emmons Glacier via a steep snow chute and ascend the glacier to 9,000 feet at the base of a large ice and snow apron on the objective face. Ascend the left end of the bergschrund apron; this could be a changing problem. Now traverse back right to the apron and climb steep snow or ice and rotten ledges, left and up to the east end of a prominent midface rock band. Now climb left upwards over snow terraces and rock bands to the pinnacle at the base of the summit cliff. The east end of the summit ridge can be attained up a vertical pitch of loose rock; start from the notch between the pinnacle and the summit ridge, then work around to complete the climb by the normal route. Grade III or IV. Bring ice screws and rock pitons.

Eric Simonson on the first winter ascent of the north face of Little Tahoma *(George Dunn)*

North Face, Simonson/Dunn variation: This climb was done in two days by Eric Simonson and George Dunn in well-iced conditions, 20 years after the first ascent. On January 7, 1979, the pair climbed from Paradise to a camp at 8,500 feet on the Ingraham Glacier. The next day they ascended the Ingraham Glacier to get around the end of the West Ridge of Little Tahoma, then descended the Emmons Glacier to the base of the North Face. The North Face climb, descent via the normal route to the Ingraham camp and subsequent descent to Paradise, took the rest of the day. The pair used a 300-foot-long 9mm rope to make long pitches.

From the bergschrund at about 9,500 feet on the Emmons Glacier, the route (right of the 1959 route) ascends two pitches to the top of a prominent snow-ice face, moving to the left onto a small rock rib. The third pitch is difficult, around a corner and up broken and iced rock. The fourth pitch traverses left then up a steep ice gully that becomes a rotten chimney to a belay atop a boulder. The fifth pitch climbs up and left over mixed terrain. The sixth pitch traverses farther left, then ascends through a prominent rock band via a steep, ice-choked gully.

Now the route starts working back to the right and up for two more pitches on ice. The ninth pitch climbs through another steep rock band where it is about 30 feet high, necessitating some hooking with ice tools. The tenth pitch continues up the upper ice fields to the ridge. Grade IV or harder. The descent was made by traversing across the upper part of the Northeast Face to the normal route, then down to the Ingraham Glacier and to Paradise.

Northeast Face, 1959

This face rises out of the upper Fryingpan Glacier, to the north of the East Shoulder, then on to the summit. There is potential rockfall danger. First ascent by Lex Maxwell, Dave Mahre, and Bob McCall on August 23, 1959.

From Summerland ascend to Fryingpan Glacier at about 7,500 feet. Traverse it northwesterly to beyond K's Spire at the northeastern foot of Little Tahoma. A number of crevasses may have to be crossed or detoured. The route then ascends the objective face, climbing through the major rock band at the 9,500-foot-level to a hanging ice patch. On the northwest skyline, note two small towers; these may be passed on either side to reach a difficult 80-foot rock pitch leading to the east summit ridge. Make a 300-foot traverse on the south flank; climb three small pinnacles to attain the summit. Grade IV; bring ice screws and rock pitons. Time: Nine hours.

Opposite: George Dunn negotiates difficult terrain on the north face of Little Tahoma. *(Eric Simonson)*

Craig Van Hoy celebrates his 100th ascent of Mount Rainier. *(Jason Edwards)*

Ingraham and Nisqually Glaciers

	Route	I	II	III	IV	V
1.	Disappointment Cleaver	•	•			
2.	Ingraham Glacier	•	•			
3.	Gibraltar Ledge, Post-1948 Route	•	•			
4.	Nisqually–Gibraltar Chute, 1946			•		
5.	Nisqually Icecliff, 1962			•		
6.	Nisqually Icefall, 1948			•	•	
7.	Nisqually Cleaver, 1967			•	•	
8.	Fuhrer Finger, 1920	•				
9.	Fuhrer Thumb, 1972	•				
10.	Wilson Headwall, 1957	•	•			

Southern and Western Flanks

	Route	I	II	III	IV	V
11.	Kautz Glacier, 1920	•				
12.	Kautz Headwall, 1963			•	•	
13.	Kautz Cleaver, 1957		•			
14.	Success Glacier Couloir, 1960		•			
15.	Middle Finger of Success, 1987		•			
16.	Fickle Finger of Success, 1997		•			
17.	Success Cleaver, 1905		•			
18.	South Tahoma Headwall, Central Route, 1963				•	
19.	South Tahoma Headwall, Western Route, 1982				•	
20.	Tahoma Cleaver, 1959				•	
21.	Tahoma Glacier, 1891		•			
22.	Sunset Amphitheater–Tahoma Glacier Icecap, 1937			•	•	
23.	Sunset Amphitheater Headwall, 1965			•	•	
24.	Sunset Ridge, 1938				•	

Mowich Face

	I	II	III	IV	V
25. Edmunds Headwall, 1957				•	•
26. Central Mowich Face, 1966				•	•
27. North Mowich Headwall, 1968				•	
28. North Mowich Face Icefall, 1970				•	

Ptarmigan to Liberty Ridges

	I	II	III	IV	V
29. Ptarmigan Ridge				•	
30. Ptarmigan Ridge–Liberty Cap Glacier, 1956			•	•	
31. Liberty Wall–Liberty Cap Glacier, 1968				•	
32. Liberty Wall Direct, 1971				•	•
33. Liberty Ridge, 1935			•	•	

Willis Wall

	I	II	III	IV	V
34. Thermogenesis, 1978				•	•
35. Willis Wall, West Rib (Damocles Rib or Brumal Buttress), 1961				•	•
36. Willis Wall, Central Rib (Agricola Rib), 1965				•	•
37. Willis Wall, East Rib (Prometheus Rib), 1963				•	
38. Willis Wall, East Face, 1962				•	

Curtis Ridge to Emmons Glacier

	I	II	III	IV	V
39. Curtis Ridge, 1957				•	
40. Western Russell Cliff, 1960		•	•		
41. Central Russell Cliff, 1973		•	•		
42. Eastern Russell Cliff, 1974		•	•		
43. Emmons and Winthrop Glaciers, 1884	•	•			

Little Tahoma

	I	II	III	IV	V
44. East Shoulder, 1894	•				
45. Other Routes					
South Face, 1991				•	
West Ridge, 1981					•
North Face, 1959 and 1979				•	•
Northeast Face, 1959				•	

Index

Climber's Notes
Ingraham and Nisqually Glaciers

Curtis Ridge to Emmons Glacier

Fred Beckey

For more than forty years, climber Fred Beckey has defined motivation. Legendary for both his tremendous appetite for first ascents, as well as his influence as a guidebook author and historian, Fred has documented and opened up most of Washington's Cascade Range.

Fred Beckey and Nancy Savickas hug to stay warm in a cool mist.

Alex Van Steen

Alex Van Steen is a guide on Mount Rainier and has guided on Everest and other mountains worldwide. He is intimately familiar with all flanks of Rainier. Highly respected for his knowledge of routes and their conditions, he has made 125 ascents to the summit by 15 different routes. He makes his home at the base of the mountain in Eatonville with his wife, Ruth Ann.

Enjoying the steep sandstone of Levitation 29 at Red Rocks near Las Vegas
(Heather Macdonald)